Endorsements

Bestselling authors Dr. Yonggi Cho and Dr. Wayde Goodall discuss how to have believing faith while encouraging us to have more faith and challenging us to believe and trust God for His leading in our lives. The amazing stories of Dr. Cho's life and the miraculous growth of the Yoido Full Gospel Church in Seoul, Korea, are thrilling. *Faith: Believing in the God Who Works on Your Behalf* offers sound biblical principles and personal stories that will certainly bring hope and inspiration to believers and skeptics alike. I encourage you to pick up your copy today!

—Dr. George Wood, general superintendent
of the Assemblies of God; chairman of the
World Assemblies of God Fellowship

In the last hundred years of the global Christian church, no one has more visibly shown how abundant faith and obedient vision can empower a leader to transition with his people from an impoverished situation to tremendous success spiritually as Yonggi Cho. This book, in which Dr. Cho and Dr. Wayde Goodall share their tested faith encounters and pilgrimage as they have trusted God for results, is most amazing and inspiring. The biblical principles gleaned from the application of promises from God's Word are contagious, encouraging the reader to step out in faith and believe God. I wholeheartedly recommend *Faith* for those who want to be used radically to further Jesus' kingdom.

—Dr. Tom Phillips, vice president,
Billy Graham Evangelistic Association

Since 1982, I have had numerous occasions to be with Dr. Cho and Yoido Full Gospel Church. The presence of the Lord has always been significant, and Dr. Cho has continued to be a friend, a great Christian leader, and an obedient servant of the Lord. His ministry has impacted the church worldwide with many Christian leaders finding their own faith increasing through the encouragement and inspiration of this special servant of God.

Dr. Wayde Goodall has written an excellent book providing new insights about a pastor and world leader who has helped shape the church in the last half of the twentieth century and first decade of this one. May these stories of faith encourage others to trust God and take steps of obedience in their own spiritual walk as Dr. David Yonggi Cho has done for over six decades.

—RUSS TOURNEY, regional director,
Asia Pacific Assemblies of God World Missions

Dr. Wayde Goodall has put his faith, years of experience, and Bible insights into a wonderful message from the greatest church of the twentieth century. Working with Dr. Cho from Soul Korea, Wayde takes us on a miraculous journey of relationship with Jesus. The Yoido Full Gospel Church and its founding pastor have brought hope and faith to millions of people around the world. With close to one million members, it truly is a supernatural experience. The stories, prayers, and Bible revelations of *Faith: Believing in the God Who Works on Your Behalf* will inspire and empower you to a greater walk with God. The real testimonies of Dr. Cho are expressed in a relevant and life-changing way through Wayde's perspectives. If you want to grow in your closeness to God and in your faith in Him, you'll love this book. Get ready for an exciting journey of faith!

—DR. CASEY TREAT, pastor,
Christian Faith Center, Seattle, WA

Dr. Yonggi Cho has blessed the world with a godly ministry that has touched the lives of countless millions. For many decades, ministers of the gospel from every denomination have looked up to Yonggi Cho as the great icon and example of church growth. I have been privileged to receive from and to associate with God's humble servant for many years. Through his church, his conferences, and his books and tapes, Yonggi Cho has been a true blessing to my life and to the lives of other pastors.

—EVANGELIST DAG HEWARD-MILLS, Healing Jesus Campaign, Accra, Ghana; founder and presiding Bishop of the Lighthouse Chapel International; graduate of the University of Ghana Medical School; Adelaide Heward-Mills conference speaker

This book by Dr. Yonggi Cho and Dr. Wayde Goodall will inspire you to a deeper level of faith. After reading *Faith: Believing in the God Who Works on Your Behalf,* you will believe God for even greater things. The principles of faith and courage will help you conquer life's challenges and experience a life of greater fulfillment. I recommend this book for anyone who desires a life of greater power and purpose.

—HAL DONALDSON, president, Convoy of Hope

It has been my privilege to serve alongside Dr. Cho for more than forty years through our involvement in Church Growth International (CGI) and the Pentecostal World Fellowship (PWF). I have been personally impacted by his life of faith as he not only teaches and preaches but also lives by example. This book about his life of faith will certainly give hope for every challenging situation.

—REV. DR. PRINCE GUNERATNAM, senior pastor of Calvary Church, Kuala Lumpur, Malaysia; general superintendent emeritus of the Assemblies of God of Malaysia; chairman of the Pentecostal World Fellowship

No one more than Reverend Dr. Cho has brought a phenomenal impact on the Body of Christ both in Korea and worldwide by proclaiming the power of the Holy Spirit through prayer in faith. I am thrilled to see how this marvelous book by the honorable Reverend Dr. Goodall and honorable Reverend Dr. Cho will touch many souls who are devoted to Jesus Christ.

—BILLY KIM, chairman of Far East Broadcasting Company, Korea; former president of Baptist World Alliance

We have been privileged to live in a period of history that has celebrated the largest known Christian church in the history of Christendom. This church has not just held that reputation for a year or two but for many, many years. The leader of this astonishing miracle and fifty-plus-year revival is Dr. Cho. What an amazing honor it is to have his life-story of faith, obedience, sacrifice, and enormously influential ministry in our hands. Like his life, this book will bring insight and impartation to so many millions of ministries, leaders, and Christians around the world. Thank you, Dr. Cho, for your incredibly inspiring life and for your generosity in sharing it in these pages.

—PHIL PRINGLE, C3 Church, Australia

I have come to know Dr. Cho as a friend, and I respect him tremendously, not only for what he has done for the Body of Christ but also for his worldwide teaching on faith in God—the God who works on our behalf. It is so important to have dreams and goals to succeed in anything in life, whether in ministry or the workplace. This book by Dr. Cho and Dr. Wayde Goodall will give you greater understanding on how to bring heaven to earth in every situation. It will help you grow in your faith and not give up on the dreams and desires God gives you. May this book empower the Body of Christ.

—REV. DR. MARGARET COURT, AO, MBE, senior pastor, Victory Life Centre, Perth, Western Australia

It is without equivocation that I recommend this book by Dr. Cho and Dr. Goodall to every believer. Whether you're a new Christian to the faith or a life disciple of our Lord who has faced challenges that deplete the soul, this book, *Faith: Believing in the God Who Works on Your Behalf*, is for you.

Faith is essential to every believer. Learning to develop faith, depend on the Holy Spirit, and practice what we learn is a lifetime achievement. I personally know no other man more than Dr. Cho who has the ability to impart faith through life lessons from his daily walk with Christ, through his personal stories of healing, and through successful achievements after overcoming tremendous odds. You will be inspired, gain practical insights, and witness your faith increase as you read the words from these pages.

In the spring of 1986, Dr. Cho took me under his wing and since then has been my pastor, mentor, and dear friend. Since 1987, I have had the honor of ministering with him in India, Africa, and other locations. He has changed my life. This book will change yours.

—DICK BERNAL, founder/pastor, Jubilee Christian Center,
San Jose, California

It has been my privilege to be a personal friend of both authors of *Faith: Believing in the God Who Works on Your Behalf.* I believe the times in which we live demand words from such great men of the period. Both Wayde Goodall and Yonggi Cho have excelled in their fields for many years. It is comforting to hear from people who have actually lived and experienced a life of faith. I highly recommend the reading of this vital work.

—DR. JOHN BUENO, former executive director of Assemblies of God
World Missions; founder of Latin America Child Care

Faith

*Believing in
the God Who Works
on Your Behalf*

YONGGI CHO
& WAYDE GOODALL

BroadStreet
PUBLISHING

BroadStreet Publishing Group, LLC
Racine, Wisconsin, USA
BroadStreetPublishing.com

Faith: Believing in the God Who Works on Your Behalf

Stock or custom editions of BroadStreet Publishing titles may be purchased in bulk for educational, business, ministry, fundraising, or sales promotional use. For information, please e-mail info@broadstreetpublishing.com.

Cover design by Chris Garborg at garborgdesign.com
Typesetting by Katherine Lloyd at theDESKonline.com

Printed in the United States of America

17 18 19 20 21 5 4 3 2 1

CONTENTS

FOREWORD

by Dr. Yong Hoon Lee

I was born and raised as a fourth-generation Presbyterian. In April 1964, my Presbyterian grandfather started attending the Full Gospel Church and invited me to that congregation. Since then, I have spent fifty-two years as a witness of the history of Yoido Full Gospel Church, working closely with Pastor Yonggi Cho in his fifty-eight-year ministry. I was baptized with the Holy Spirit through Pastor Cho's ministry and from him have been learning how to activate my faith. The two pillars of Pastor Cho's ministry have been faith in the fullness of the Holy Spirit and the faith armored with absolute positivity.

Pastor Cho planted a church in Daejo-dong area in Seoul with his late mother-in-law, Pastor Jashil Choi, in 1958. It was a small tent church with only five members, yet it grew rapidly and, within several years, had to move to a new sanctuary in the Seodaemun neighborhood. The church continued to grow to eighteen thousand members in nine years. In 1973, the church moved to its current location in Yoido Island. At the time of Pastor Cho's retirement in May 2008, Yoido Full Gospel Church was the largest congregation in the world, with eight hundred thousand members. All of this has been possible because God has walked with Pastor Cho in his ministry.

I believe no Korean pastor has ever matched the passion Pastor Cho has manifested in emphasizing the importance of the fullness of the Holy Spirit for the Christian life. Pastor Cho has always said, "Holy Spirit, I acknowledge, welcome, invite, and rely on you," calling him his Senior Partner in his ministry.

Pastor Cho's theology and spirituality are epitomized in the Five-fold Gospel, the Threefold Blessing, and the Fourth Dimensional Spirituality. The Fivefold Gospel describes the core five blessings manifested in the gospel of the cross of Jesus Christ: Regeneration, the Fullness of the Holy Spirit, Divine Healing, Blessing, and the Second Coming. The Threefold Blessing refers to the holistic blessing given to the believers in Jesus as a result of the atonement of the cross: "I pray that you may enjoy good health and that all may go well with you, even as your soul is getting along well" (3 John 2). The Fourth Dimensional Spirituality offers practical ways to apply the Fivefold Gospel and the Threefold Blessing to everyday life. Christians can enjoy God's blessing by using their thought, dream, faith, and language in a right way in the Holy Spirit. With the message of the Fivefold Gospel, the Threefold Blessing, and the Fourth Dimensional Spirituality, Pastor Cho has gone around the world to preach the gospel, and his ministry has impacted world Christianity.

I would like to express my sincere gratitude to Dr. Goodall for his painstaking work on this wonderful biography of my spiritual mentor and the founder of Yoido Full Gospel Church. Reviewing the ministry and theology of Pastor Cho and his great contribution to the foundation and growth of Yoido Full Gospel Church through the scholarly lens offered by an esteemed theologian is inspirational and insightful.

I hope God will be with all the readers of this wonderful book as he has worked in the life and ministry of Pastor Cho. I also pray that this book will expand the understanding of Pastor Cho's spirituality and theology, setting an example of faith for many people to see realized in their lives.

Dr. Reverend Young Hoon Lee
Senior Pastor, Yoido Full Gospel Church, South Korea
Co-president of the Christian Council of Korea
Chairman of National Council of Churches in Korea
Chairman of Assemblies of God of Korea

FOREWORD

by Dr. Dick Eastman

The hospital system in my city is currently running an advertising campaign in which survivors share their stories in simple "then-now" statements: "*Then* I suffered a massive heart attack. *Now* I climb a new mountain every month"; "*Then* I couldn't breathe. *Now* I run six miles every morning." Between *then* and *now*, we assume a story of doctors and nurses, surgeries and recoveries. Between *then* and *now* is a hospital system.

This picture came to mind as I read Dr. Yonggi Cho's story in this insightful and provocative book. *Then* Cho was a hopeless young man trapped in poverty and Buddhism in Korea, diagnosed with a fatal case of tuberculosis. *Then* he was certain he would die very soon and had nowhere to look for hope or salvation. *Now* Pastor Cho is a healthy man who has lived in the abundance of life in daily partnership with the Holy Spirit. *Now* he has given birth to what is widely considered the largest church in the world, leading a movement that has touched all corners of the planet. *Now* he has a lifetime of stories of healing and miracles to share, with some of the most amazing of these stories included in the pages that follow.

Between Pastor Cho's *then* and *now* is not a hospital system; it is a living, active, and faithful God who rescued him out of death into a life driven by eternity and marked by the miraculous. Between Cho's *then* and *now* is a life of incredible devotion, trust, faith, and belief. The book you hold in your hands is the in-between—the link between the *then* and *now* in Pastor Cho's story. It's a powerful and profound "bridge of faith" between Dr. Cho's *then* and his present day *now*. It beckons you to cross that bridge into a new and exciting realm of believing the implausible and attempting the impossible. And if your heart is open, it could well be the bridge from your *then* to an amazingly miraculous *now*. I know it has been for me.

In a somewhat unique way, I had the privilege of being a part of Dr. Cho's *then* some fifty years ago when, as a twenty-two-year-old youth pastor in southern Wisconsin, our church hosted Pastor Cho in his very first trip to America. It was the mid-1960s. I vividly recall Dr. Cho's message, shared without the aid of an interpreter, describing how he had planted a new church in Seoul, Korea, just six years earlier. Their first building was not a building at all but a tent. With a touch of humor, the thin Korean pastor told how at the starting of his church with just five believers (including the woman who was to become his mother-in-law), he asked God boldly to give him one thousand new members each year. "But God did not answer my prayer as I had prayed it," Cho explained. "Today I should have six thousand members. Instead, I have seven thousand!" The young Korean pastor smiled and added, "So, I've been asking God why he gave me a thousand too many!" On the pages of this remarkable book, you will read more details of this miracle and the many that followed.

Cho's *then* in the 1960s was preparing him for a supernaturally wonderful *now*. Indeed, if Dr. Cho had continued to see a thousand souls added to his congregation's numbers over each of those ensuing years, his church would have a remarkable fifty-seven thousand members today. But instead, Pastor Cho's *now* has grown to more than twelve times that number—exceeding eight hundred thousand members. Imagine pastoring a congregation that increased by some twelve thousand new members every year for some five decades! But there would be no *now* were it not for Cho's *then*. Pastor Cho's journey has truly been a journey of extraordinary faith lived out of countless hours spent in the secret place of prayer (often four or five hours daily).

Faith: Believing in the God Who Works on Your Behalf is truly a supernaturally anointed, faith-inspiring manual directing the reader to a wonderfully fruitful Christian life. This is, simply put, a book about how to have faith that prevails. In the pages that follow, Pastor Cho, along with a dear personal friend and ministry coworker of mine, Wayde Goodall (who serves on our ministry's international board of directors), explores what it looks like to surrender fully to a radical pursuit of Jesus Christ—living a faith-saturated life in His presence, trusting daily in the leading of the Holy Spirit, and pursuing a wonderfully fruitful personal ministry the Lord has set before each of us (with eternity in view).

If you are a Christ-follower longing to experience more of the power of God in your life, this book is for you. If you are wondering what it means to believe in Jesus at all, this book is for you. If you are a seasoned believer who already has seen miracles of the Lord in your life, this book will cause you to yearn for even more. Pastor Cho's story and Wayde Goodall's time-tested insights truly lead us into the deeper things of God. They offer tools to pursue the voice of the Holy Spirit and follow Him with reckless abandon, unafraid and—most importantly—full of genuine faith. My desire is to challenge all eight thousand of Every Home for Christ's global staff to read this incredible book at least once every year. I've made that my personal goal. If you read this book just once, you'll understand why I offer this challenge.

What is your *then*? What will be your *now*? What dreams, hopes, and plans has the Holy Spirit planted in your heart? Where might you go if you truly opened your heart to His leading? What would you do if you truly believed in the God of the Bible—a God who is full of love and power and amazing plans for your life? If any of these questions touches your heart, I invite you to plunge into these pages with your eyes wide open and your heart keenly awake. I believe the Lord wants to bridge your *then* to your *now* (and beyond) into a supernatural abundance of His Spirit. Read on and discover how.

Dr. Dick Eastman
International President, Every Home for Christ

SECTION I

Depending on the Holy Spirit

Every morning when I awake I greet the Holy Spirit and invite Him to go with me through the day and take the lead in all my affairs, and He does. I say, "Good morning, Holy Spirit. Let's work together today, and I will be your vessel." Every evening before retiring I say again, "It's been a wonderful day working with you, Holy Spirit."

—Yonggi Cho, *Holy Spirit, My Senior Partner*

1

Born Again:
How My Faith Walk Began

One thing I do know, that though I was blind, now I see.
—John 9:25 ESV

My (Dr. Cho) family lived in North Korea. When the Korean War broke out, we lost our home. And so with other refugees, we traveled south to Pusan. Money and food were extremely scarce, and I worked hard to eke out an existence of one meal a day and to continue my education.

One day while I was working, blood filled my mouth. Soon it was also coming from my nose, and I struggled to keep from choking, until finally I blacked out. When I regained consciousness, my clothing was soaked in blood. My head was spinning—I was too dizzy to stand up. I'm not certain of how long I had been there, but I knew something was terribly wrong.

I struggled to walk but managed to reach home. All during the night I was in and out of consciousness. My fever continued to rise, and when I coughed, blood gushed out of my mouth. By morning I was weak, feeling like I was more dead than alive. My parents took me to a hospital and the doctor examined me and X-rayed my chest. The doctor said, "I am sorry, but we can do nothing for you. You have less than a month to live."

"Doctor," I cried out, "are you telling me the truth?"

He showed us the X-rays and explained, "Your right lung is completely destroyed by tuberculosis. The upper part has collapsed and gangrene has set in. Your left lung is also tubercular. Malnutrition and hard work have caused your heart to enlarge, and it cannot circulate the blood properly. There is no medical help for these things, so I have no choice but to tell you the truth."

Dazed, I returned home, where my father tried to reassure me: "My son, there is no life and no death, no joy and no sorrow, only in Buddha is there reality. Forget about life and death and have peace." But no matter what he said, his logic didn't make sense to me.

"The blood that I am vomiting is real," I told my father. "My suffering is real. Buddha and your philosophies have not helped me. I reject them all."

Not long after that, I became fearful and desperate. So I cried out, "Is there any God? If there is anyone called God—anywhere in the universe—then please come and help me. I want to make myself ready to die." God heard my prayer and He answered, but in a form I didn't expect!

A young girl knocked on my door and entered. She was carrying a Bible. I was stunned because at the time, especially in our culture, women were not forward and men disliked being taught by them. Arrogantly, I ordered the girl to leave, but she said, "I can see that you are dying. I want to tell you about Christ Jesus, my Savior."

I became angry and cursed her. I told her that millions of tuberculosis germs were flying around in the air and that she would become infected. She only replied, "My Christ will protect me." She continued to witness to me before she finally left.

But the following morning she was back again. This time she sang some songs and read aloud from her Bible. I cursed and called her a Christian dog, but she did not respond to my rudeness; rather, she remained calm and persistent. For hours she talked about Christ. She did this for two more days.

When she came on the fifth day, I asked why she continued to come back and pray for me. She simply said, "There is someone who constrains me to come here and pray for you."

"Who is it?" I asked.

She gave me her Bible, and I began reading at the place she indicated—Matthew 1. After a few minutes, I said, "This is like a telephone directory. How can this help me?" She told me to keep reading and I would find a wonderful story.

After she left, I continued to read, expecting to find a difficult philosophy such as I had studied in Buddhism. But I found that the Bible was about a man called Jesus Christ, who was the Son of God! I read about Jesus healing the sick and those who were dying. I thought, *If only I could come to this Jesus. He would help me!*

In my mind, reason argued that I could not do this. I had cursed and hated Him. I tried to find a Scripture verse showing that Christ hated sinners, but search as I would, I could not find one. Instead, I found that He forgave an adulteress and delivered a demon-possessed man. He always received the sick and sinful. Slowly the realization came to me: although I was the poorest of the poor, a great sinner, and dying with tuberculosis, Jesus Christ would receive me!

I decided to pray and ask Jesus to become my Savior. A great peace showered down upon me; every cell in my body seemed charged with new life. Something began to bubble up inside. I thought at first that I was going to vomit blood again, but then I realized it was joy! I wanted to sing, but I didn't know how.

After going through a tremendous amount of rejection from my family because I had left the Buddhist faith, I rented a small room in which to live. One day, I locked the door of my room and began to pray. "Jesus," I said, "I want to meet you and have a consultation about my future." I waited, but Christ did not come. Then I shut my eyes tightly, hoping He might come in a vision. But no vision appeared. I prayed all day. By nighttime, I was soaked in perspiration, but I still prayed. After midnight, the strength had left my body and I lay down to rest.

Suddenly the room became bright. A billow of what I thought was smoke rolled in. I was awestruck. Thinking the house was on fire, I tried to call for help, but no one came. In desperation, I looked around and beside me I saw two feet. I looked up higher and saw a white robe. Then I looked into a face that was like a powerful sun and rays of light shining outward. But I still didn't know who He was until I saw the crown of thorns on His head. They were piercing His temples and the blood was streaming down His face. I knew then that He was Jesus Christ. His love seemed to pour over me.

My gods had been gods of fear and curses. I had always gone into their temples to beg them not to punish me. But Jesus was different. As I felt His love, all fear left me. Glorious joy came from my inner being. My tongue and lips began to speak. I tried to stop, but it seemed that another person was controlling them and forcefully expressing Himself through me. I did not know what it was, but I realized that the more I spoke the better I felt, and so I continued to speak.

When I became aware of my surroundings once again, Jesus had gone, but the glory was still in my soul. I forgot about the pain in my heart and lungs and ran to a nearby house where a missionary whom I had met stayed. I knew that Louis Richards, the Assemblies of God missionary, would be able to answer my questions about this experience. When I explained to him that I spoke in a strange language, he opened his Bible to Acts 2 and explained that I had been baptized with the Spirit as the early believers had. We cried and expressed our thankfulness and joy.

Some time later, I realized I was no longer suffering from heart pain or shortness of breath. I went to the hospital, and after an examination and X-rays the doctor told me that my lungs were well. No tuberculosis! Even my heart was a normal size once again.[1]

Since that time of experiencing the power and presence of the Holy Spirit, my life has been a life of walking by faith. Everything that has been accomplished in my life is because of the precious grace of God. Another has purchased me; I now belong to Jesus. To Him be the glory.

Faith in Jesus Christ will change your life forever. As you walk by faith in Him, He will help you grow in your faith and believe in miracles and signs and wonders. God will use you in amazing ways and give you courage beyond anything you could have thought was possible. The principles in this book are truths that can be applied to your life. Walk by faith, believe in the impossible, dream His dreams, and let God ...

But, as it is written,
> "What no eye has seen, nor ear heard,
>   nor the heart of man imagined,
> what God has prepared for those who love him"
> —these things God has revealed to us through the Spirit.
For the Spirit searches everything, even the depths of God.
(1 Corinthians 2:9–10 ESV)

2

Faith and Dreams

Faith is more important to me than life itself because
without it there would be no fullness of life.
—Mother Teresa

When I (Dr. Cho) was dying with terminal tuberculosis—
growing weak, coughing up blood, and thinking that my life
would soon end—I had lost all hope, and I had nowhere to turn.
My family's Buddhist beliefs brought me no hope for life or healing, no answers to the questions of what would happen after death.
Although I didn't understand prayer, I prayed, "Lord, if you heal
me, I will give the rest of my life to you and I'll become a minister."
After that, I noticed that I was feeling better and had more energy.
In six months, I was so healthy that I could breathe normally once
again. Although they could not explain it, the doctors told me, "You
are healed."

When I gave my life to Jesus Christ, my faith was simple. My
miracle was an obvious sign to me that Jesus still healed. I began
the discipline of prayer and studying the Scriptures. I grew in my
understanding of miracles, how prayers are answered, and how God
often gives dreams and visions to His children. I believed in what
the Holy Spirit had revealed to me, and I had hope when there was

no hope. By faith I could see things happening when they were not yet in existence in this physical world. I thought and imagined that what I was praying about was actually possible. With the dreams the Holy Spirit gave me, I believed that with Christ all these things were truly possible.

Because of what I understood the Bible had to say about healing, as well as my own personal experience of being healed, I developed the faith that others could receive healing too. Over many years of serving Jesus Christ, I have witnessed countless miracles, signs, and wonders. As a young Christian, I wasn't certain about how this happened, but I now anticipate miracles and the wonderful healings that come when we pray by faith and believe.

Positive Dreams Give Hope

The Bible tells us that all of us have a "measure of faith" (Romans 12:3 KJV). Even though our faith is as small as a mustard seed, Jesus said it could grow into a huge tree (Matthew 17:20). Faith grows as we pray and meditate on God's Word and on His goodness (see Joshua 1:8; Psalm 119:15–16; John 15:7). With the help of the Holy Spirit, we can discipline ourselves to think about the positive and the good (Philippians 4:8) promises from Scripture. As we do this, our thoughts are positive. When our thoughts are positive, we are able to think of what is possible and not the impossible. We experience dreams and have visions that give us hope.

Hope is a tremendous experience that gives us a renewed endurance and strength. The enemy would like to take your hope and discourage you because he knows that your faith will be greatly weakened as a result. Jesus Christ gives us hope, and as we walk by faith, our hope will only continue to grow.

All followers of Jesus Christ have dreams, but because of their lack of faith, many do not believe their dreams are possible. Fear, discouragement, worry, and obsessing about rejection are all enemies of faith. Anger, bitterness, sinful thinking, and the attack of the enemy can cause a person's mind to be preoccupied with negative or sinful thoughts. These thoughts can become debilitating and overwhelming at times.

People who have been terribly hurt, abused, or experienced terrible trauma often have painful memories from their past that continually influence their thoughts. The Lord is the healer; even though we might have tragic memories, the emotional pain can be removed.[1] We can experience this miracle as we let our minds be transformed by the Word of God (Romans 12:1–2), with God's help forgive those who have hurt us, and permit the Holy Spirit to give us peace from our past.

We can discipline ourselves to find a way to focus our thoughts on the goodness of God, on the beautiful, the positive, and what is truthful and pure (Philippians 4:8). As a child of God, we decide to control our time (so we can pray and meditate on God's Word), and our minds will naturally hear the gentle voice of the Holy Spirit in that quietness. It is here where our positive dreams infuse us with hope.

The truth is that all of us have hopes, dreams, and visions. Many incredible inventions, programs, companies, churches, careers, personal goals, and dreams have been accomplished because of this God-given ability. For the Christ-follower, we pray and meditate on God's Word, and as we listen to the voice of the Holy Spirit, we frequently have a growing desire or vision of what we can do. Mother Teresa said, "Reach high, for stars lie hidden in your soul. Dream deep, for every dream precedes the goal."[2]

When we have a dream or a vision, or we imagine a solution to a situation, we must ask ourselves: Does this have a biblical precedent? Does it line up with experiences cited in the Word of God? As humans, we are capable of compromising, rationalizing, and justifying bad and sinful behaviors, but we need to keep our own thoughts in check. God invites us to examine all our behaviors, desires, thoughts, and dreams by what Scripture tells us is true or false. If we can support our thoughts by the truth that is found in the Word, then we can process how to plan our next step and believe by faith.

Dreams Give Hope for Tomorrow

A dream that is given by the Holy Spirit refers to the hopes and wishes for tomorrow. This inspired thought can be about us or about our family members and friends. It can be about our occupation, strategies of how to do what is on our heart, or a multitude of other possibilities. God is a creative God who can give us a creative idea that can open the door to circumstances that will bless our lives and the lives of those who are important to us. We carry the dream in our hearts.

People who are successful are, without exception, people who have dreamed. They see what others do not see. Oftentimes they stand alone with their confidence and vision. Henry David Thoreau once said, "I have learned, that if one advances confidently in the direction of his dreams, and endeavors to live the life he has imagined, he will meet with a success unexpected in common hours."[3]

At the age of seventy-five, Abraham received God's calling when he was in Ur of the Chaldeans and he carried the dream that God gave to him. Although he was asked to leave the place he knew and go to a place where he had no guarantees, Abraham possessed his dream. He carried that dream in his heart and continued to pray about the dream he was given. God answered his prayer and made him into the father of faith (Genesis 12–24; Romans 4).

Abraham's great-grandson Joseph had two dreams that were misunderstood by his family. Even he didn't understand the meaning of the dreams as he saw himself leading his brothers. When he told his brothers about his dream, they were threatened by the possibility that he would become greater than they. In fact, they thought his dream was his pride and arrogance; as a result, they were so angry with him that they wanted to kill him (Genesis 37).

Principles of Faith and Dreams

When you begin to believe that God can speak to you and give you thoughts, dreams, and visions, then *your life will change because you will have brought Jesus Christ into the equation.* This wonderful truth has changed everything I (Dr. Cho) do as I endeavor to ask the Holy Spirit to be my partner in daily life. When I sense that the Holy Spirit is giving me a dream or a vision, I study and understand principles that the Scriptures give, then I think through a process and move forward by faith. Here are some of the principles of faith and dreams that I understand.

A Dream Is Not yet a Reality

God has a future and a hope for each one of us. He doesn't tell us 100 percent of our future, but as we study God's Word, pray, and meditate on His truths, God will speak to us about the future and the plans He has for us. This is an experience that gives us hope, imparting to us tremendous amounts of strength and energy. Although the dream is only in our mind and not yet a reality, we can begin to pray, examine this idea from Scripture, and think about the process of how to begin acting by faith in the implementation of the dream.

Throughout the Bible, God has frequently showed godly people His own perspective on the times and conditions in which they live. He has shown His perspective on what is going on and has revealed His purposes and actions. Men and women of God have frequently interpreted events accurately for God's people: "For the LORD God does nothing without revealing his secret to his servants the prophets" (Amos 3:7 ESV).

Frequently, I (Dr. Cho) refrain from telling anyone about my dream or vision when I first receive it. Before sharing it with anyone, I think about it (sometimes for weeks, months, or even years). When a dream is from the Holy Spirit, it grows and develops. More ideas will come as we meditate on what the Lord has given to us. But I *specifically pray* about the dream and ask the Holy Spirit for a strategy and for His favor (Proverbs 16:3). I compare the dream to what the Bible says, holding it in my heart.

When the shepherds spoke to Mary, the mother of Jesus, she "treasured up all these things, pondering them in her heart" (Luke 2:19 ESV). Many times, it is wise to place our dream on a shelf in our heart, holding it there as we receive more clarification of the details or the timing. If I sense the Holy Spirit has given me a dream, I know it is not yet reality; however, it provides a goal for which I can strive. Goals are important and need to be written down and specifically prayed about as we process how to accomplish what God has put in our hearts.

If we don't have a dream, then we no goals to live by and can become fatalistic minded. Then it becomes easy for us to fall into despair when difficulties come our way. Having a dream and walking by faith as we move forward is frequently filled with many challenges, which are nothing more than opportunities to trust God and permit Him to help us with difficult people or situations.

Even though we are experiencing a difficult challenge or trial, or have made a mistake, we have hope God will show us how to turn our difficulty into His "good purpose." Paul reminds us that "it is God who works in you to will and to act in order to fulfill his good purpose" (Philippians 2:13). We need to be willing to walk away from any experience that has discouraged us and weakened our strength. Instead, we choose to look at the wonderful possibilities the Lord brings into our lives. With God's help, we can refuse to let our past failures, heartaches, rejections, attacks from the enemy, or negative comments from people rob us from His good purposes in our lives.

Don't let a mistake or falling into doubt prevent you from starting over again. One of your greatest challenges is to fail to begin again when you doubt. Don't worry, because God will help you and believes that you can do all that He has given you to do. He is with you and you are competent in Christ. Like Paul, we declare, "But one thing I do, forgetting what is behind and straining toward what is ahead, I press on toward the goal to win the prize for which God has called me heavenward in Christ Jesus" (Philippians 3:13–14).

Although our dreams are not yet a reality, they can give us vision to accomplish God's will and His purpose in our lives. It is important to structure our lives as we prioritize our time and energy, so we can pray. As we pray, we plan how to develop our goals and the strategies to accomplish our vision.

If we feel the Holy Spirit has given us an idea or a solution, we can process how to accomplish this endeavor. If the busyness of life has conflicted with the time you spend in prayer and listening to the Holy Spirit, then free up your time today. Don't let the mistakes or lack of discipline from yesterday paralyze you from what the Lord has for you today. If you don't control your time, then someone else will.

To hope under the most extreme circumstances is
an act of defiance that permits a person to live his life
on his own terms. It is part of the human spirit to
endure and give a miracle a chance to happen.

—Jerome Groopman, *The Anatomy of Hope*

As a young Christian, I considered becoming a professor but soon felt I was to become a pastor. With that dream, I began my first church in a tent with Jashil Choi (my future mother-in-law) and her three children in a poor slum area of Seoul, Korea. This was shortly after the Korean War—the community was destitute, people were poor and without hope, and many were sick. Although there were only five of us, in my heart I saw the tent full of people.

I believed that God could give people hope, so my messages included being filled with the Spirit, healing, and giving my listeners courage and faith. I believed and preached that poor people could find jobs and healing for lives that were broken. Because of what the Lord had done in my own life, I knew God could change their lives too. Many miracles happened and people's lives changed as they came to Christ. There were many people who believed, and many more had miraculous and healing experiences.

In about three years, the church attendance was around three hundred precious people. Because these people received hope in Jesus Christ, they told their families, friends, and neighbors about what was happening at church. As a result, many came to hear of God's possibilities. Hope is a desperate need; when people discover hope, they become a magnet to their friends and family.

When our first church location had hundreds of people, it was obvious we needed a different location that would give us the ability to build a building that would accommodate many more people. I found land available in an area called Seodaemun. My dream was to build a great church that allowed thousands to attend and hear the truth about Jesus Christ proclaimed. By faith, the Seodaemun church was built. In approximately seven years, this congregation increased to many thousands.

We began cell groups that met in the different parts of the city as we divided Seoul into twenty zones. We trained leaders, encouraged their faith, and mentored them so they could hold services for worship and Bible study in their homes throughout the week. They invited their non-Christian friends, neighbors, and people with whom they worked. As the various cell groups grew, the leaders trained others to lead a group when their group divided because of its size.

My dream had become a reality. But it wasn't long before I knew that we needed to move again to a larger facility. I envisioned tens of thousands of people. In my heart I saw masses of people coming to the church and receiving hope, healing, and restoration. I needed to pray and listen for the Holy Spirit to give me details, courage, favor, and a sense of timing. The future building and different ministries came to my thoughts as I listened.

The economic depression of that time, the opposition, hardships, and struggles could have easily brought discouragement and caused us to give up. There were times when I was overwhelmed with discouragement and didn't know what to do. Many thought it couldn't be done. Human advice could not bring hope. But I continued to focus on prayer, reading and meditating on God's Word, listening to the Holy Spirit, and believing that with Christ "all things are possible" (Matthew 19:26). God would bring the solution in the right time.

We built and implemented what God had given to me through a dream in my heart. The new facility holds twelve thousand with other facilities that enable us to minister to thirty-four thousand people. The membership of the Yoido church reached a hundred thousand people in approximately six years, then two hundred thousand about a year later, and then five hundred thousand within the next five years. In just a few more years, we had seven hundred thousand people! The church has continued to grow as we have prayed and preached the message of hope.

With each dream the Holy Spirit gave to me, I prayed and planned. My dream developed into a goal that needed to be acted on. If I only kept the dream from the Holy Spirit in my mind, and not acted on it, then little would have been accomplished for Christ.

A frequent experience that can be a part of our prayers is that when we pray, we need to see a sick person well, a business plan working, a complicated situation becoming healthy, or a marriage healed. We are encouraged to believe that these thoughts could very well be God-inspired thoughts, which can then be turned into faith. Pray about how to implement a strategy to work with God to bring that thought to pass.

Your dream is not yet a reality. But as you pray and meditate on the Scripture, you can begin setting goals and ways to implement your goals. Mary Kay Ash said, "An average person with average talents and ambition and average education can outstrip the most brilliant genius in our society, if that person has clear, focused goals."[4] How much more is that true when we bring Jesus into the equation!

A Dream Is Like a Wish in Your Mind

We like to think that a dream is like a wish drawn on the canvas of our hearts. All of us have "wishes." People who have a wish (or a dream) can look at their dream and be thankful to God as they pray about their desire. What is a wish? A wish is defined as a "desire for something to happen or be done: a feeling of wanting to do or have something."[5]

When God spoke to Abraham, Abraham had a new dream in his heart for the future. This became a desire (or a wish), and he was filled with hope. Although he didn't understand the details of the dream, he believed what God had shown him. He didn't rely upon his human strength or wealth, but trusted in what God had promised. This promise became part of the dream in his heart. He had hope and felt encouraged to do what God had given him to do. The writer of Hebrews tells us, "By faith Abraham obeyed when he was called to go out to a place that he was to receive as an inheritance. And he went out, not knowing where he was going" (Hebrews 11:8 ESV).

Through hearing from God and the dreams that He had given

him, insurmountable faith was birthed in Abraham's heart. His dream became a wish (a desire), and Abraham left Ur of the Chaldeans. By faith he walked away from what he knew, all because of the dream that he would receive an inheritance per God's promise. As Abraham likely felt alone, many times we too feel alone. But we must remind ourselves that our creator God is with us, never leaving us or forsaking us.

When Abraham was ninety-nine years old, he had faith to have his own natural-born child. His faith came because of the promise that God had given him, that then became a desire to have a son. Like us, he doubted and wondered, *How can a man who is almost a hundred years old produce a child?* God had clearly told him that he would have a son. In the natural, it wasn't possible because of his age, but with God added into the equation his dream became a reality and his son Isaac was born.

Abraham believed. He trusted in God and believed that God would fulfill His promise even though he didn't completely understand how it would come about. With that hope, he took his first step by faith and walked away from his past. Paul writes of Abraham's faith in Romans:

> He did not weaken in faith when he considered his own body, which was as good as dead (since he was about a hundred years old), or when he considered the barrenness of Sarah's womb. No unbelief made him waver concerning the promise of God, but he grew strong in his faith as he gave glory to God. (4:19–20 ESV)

When we have faith and the dream that the Holy Spirit has planted in our minds, and we begin thinking, planning, and processing, then our hope grows as we step out in faith. Our mind changes from doubt to faith as we experience the evidence of what is in our heart actually coming to pass. Jerome Groopman confirms this in his book *The Anatomy of Hope*: "Researchers are learning that a change in mind-set has the power to alter neurochemistry. Belief and expectation—the key elements of hope—can block pain by releasing the brain's endorphins and enkephalins, mimicking the effects of morphine."[6]

Abraham prayed many years for a son. He had been promised that he would have as many descendants as the stars in the sky. On the clear nights, he could see tens of thousands of stars. They seemed to be unending. As Abraham gazed at the stars, his imagination grew, encouragement filled him, and the anticipation of the fulfilled dream was his frequent thought. This filled him with hope.

When we have a dream that the Holy Spirit has placed in our hearts, we can pray and trust that God hears our prayers and will give us wisdom and patience as He brings our dream to fruition. But this will only happen in His time.

A Dream Makes the Impossible Possible

When Moses and the children of Israel were on the edge of the Promised Land, Moses appointed twelve men to go into Canaan to observe the people, describe the kinds of food there, and to bring back a report. To the surprise of Moses, ten out of the twelve spies came back with a report full of fear and defeat. The obstacles seemed impossible as fear and concern overcame them. The obstacles were problems that seemed too big; in fact, they felt the situation was impossible. Fear replaced faith and trust.

They had a humanistic perspective. They only looked at the impossibilities of their circumstances; consequently, they lost their dream of living in the land of Canaan (Numbers 13:31–33). When they lost their dream, they lost their hope that it could be done. And so they felt like *grasshoppers* among *giants*.

Joshua and Caleb saw the same situation but had a different opinion from the other ten men. They gathered the same information, considered the same situation and the environment, and saw the same giants—but Caleb and Joshua had a different attitude. They said, "We can do it" (Numbers 14:6–9).

Joshua and Caleb knew that it would be done with God's help. As they observed the land, the obstacles, and the giants, they saw the possibilities. They had seen God's deliverance before and knew that He would miraculously help them once again. They were not discouraged in their faith; rather, they were motivated and determined as they trusted God to do what He had promised. Joshua and Caleb never lost their dream.

Some have the faith of grasshoppers while others have faith in God. Faith from God is an active, positive faith that trusts Him to bring the needed help and favor to accomplish what He said He would do.

The Bible is full of God's promises, about 3,500 of them. Herbert Lockyer wrote a book called *All the Promises of the Bible* and claims to list eight thousand promises from God. No matter which number you go with, the truth is that there are thousands of promises contained in God's Word. The point of God giving us promises is to help us believe that they can be part of our day-to-day lives. Believing and acting on the promises of God is acknowledging that what seems impossible is possible. Jesus said, "With God, all things are possible" (Matthew 19:26 ESV).

When Jesus asked His disciples, "Where can we buy bread for all these people?" Philip answered that they would need about two hundred denarii[7] worth of bread to feed all the people present that day (John 6:5–7). He answered in this logical way because he wasn't thinking of Jesus, who brings about miracles and change, but about how they couldn't get what they needed from a natural source (buying bread).

Andrew had a different thought. He told Jesus what resources were available (five loaves of bread and two fish). Perhaps he believed that with Jesus in the equation, there just might be a way that all the people could be fed. That day Jesus performed the miracle of feeding five thousand men, plus the women and the children, with just five loaves of bread and two fish (John 6:8–9).

Fourth-Dimensional Spirituality

To fulfill our dreams and accomplish the vision that is in our hearts, we must apply what I (Dr. Cho) have called "fourth-dimensional spirituality" to our lives. We typically interact with height, width, and depth (three dimensions), although science has discovered that there are many more dimensions in our universe. When I speak about *fourth-dimensional spirituality*, I am reminding us that there is a spiritual—supernatural—world beyond the three dimensions we typically live in and of which we are aware. Our Creator can give us visions, dreams, and wonderful plans that are far beyond the physical dimensions in which we live.

When we carry a dream in our hearts, we believe that change will come and God will bring about the necessary miracles. We then move ahead with creative proclamations from our lips that are positive and not driven by fear. God will work with us to fulfill the dreams He gives us. Decades ago, I only imagined what God could do; now I see what God has done and is still doing.

What is the dream or vision that you sense the Holy Spirit has given you? With God's help, you can do it. Remember to apply the principles of faith as you begin to step out in faith. If you are full of doubt, then make the decision that one day at a time you will read the Scriptures, pray, and listen. Specifically talk to God about your requests and needs. Ask Him to be your partner. The voice of the Holy Spirit will come to your thoughts as you clear your mind. Work with God in accomplishing your Holy Spirit-inspired thoughts and dreams. And continue to remind yourself that you are not alone or living empty-handed. Together, with Jesus, you can do it.

3

Being Led by the Spirit

There is only one way to live your everyday life, and that is
with your faith and your hope permanently on God.
—Billy Graham

As believers, it is our desire to please and glorify God in all that
we do. We want to do His will and be what He wants us to be.
However, when we read statements like this, it is likely that most of
us frequently wonder how we can know the will of God, and if it is
even possible. But for a combined total of over ninety years, we (Dr.
Cho and Wayde) have been followers of Jesus Christ. We've discovered that dreams, visions, and circumstances are frequently a part
of how God directs us as we move forward by faith.

As a young Christian, missionaries greatly encouraged me (Dr.
Cho) to go to a small seminary in Seoul. I insatiably studied as
I've always had a deep hunger to read, study, and research. I read
most of the books on the shelves of the small library. At the time,
I thought that I would become a seminary professor; however, the
Lord had other plans. When I had finished my seminary education,
another student (Jashil Choi, 최자실) and I pioneered the church at
Bulgwang-Dong (now Daejo-Dong), which met in a tent.

In those days, we prayed no less than ten hours a day. There was nothing else to do but pray. Most of the village people who moved from the country were living in board-framed houses. They were reduced to beggarly conditions. As I prayed for many hours every day, I became so hoarse that I couldn't even speak after prayer. I poured all my strength into crying out to God. It was said that people could hear my prayers in the bus station, which was located a fair distance from the hill where the tent church stood. At four thirty each morning, I began to cry out until seven o'clock, and after breakfast, if there were no people to visit, I prayed until noon. After another break, I prayed until evening and did not go home because I had no house.

Most of our congregation didn't have houses either, so we all lived together in the tent church. Because we were so poor, we didn't have entertainment or other distractions that hindered our times of prayer. We had no television, no radio or cell phones, and no money to visit the theater. We could only pray; and so we prayed with fervor and determination.

The fire of the Holy Spirit began to fall on us as we continued to pray. Miracles, signs, and wonders became part of our little church. Demons were cast out and diseases were healed. Then the crippled and the lame were healed. At that time, when I prayed more than ten hours a day, I saw the biggest miracles in my life. As a result, in three years the congregation grew to hundreds of people who had experienced God.[1]

Through this experience of witnessing signs and wonders (that were certainly influenced by prayer), I perceived the reality of *planting and harvesting in the spiritual realm*, much like farmers do in the natural realm. I knew that miracles only take place through God according to our faith—not by chance or random circumstances.

Walking in the Spirit means we walk by faith. We can't see the Holy Spirit with our physical eyes, but we can develop our sensitivity to His voice and promptings. There are many areas in our lives where we need to trust God and decide to wait for His encouragement to move forward, to stop, or to change direction. The example of the Holy Spirit opening and closing doors, giving visions, and, as a result, moving forward by faith is given to us in Acts 16:

> Paul and his companions traveled throughout the region of Phrygia and Galatia, *having been kept by the Holy Spirit* from preaching the word in the province of Asia. When they came to the border of Mysia, they tried to enter Bithynia, but the *Spirit of Jesus would not allow them to.* So they passed by Mysia and went down to Troas. During the night *Paul had a vision* of a man of Macedonia standing and begging him, "Come over to Macedonia and help us." After *Paul had seen the vision, we got ready at once* to leave for Macedonia, *concluding that God had called us to preach the gospel to them.* (vv. 6–11)

How Do We Know What to Do?

It's not right to simply talk about *an experience* when we communicate about the Holy Spirit. The Holy Spirit is a person; we should have deep fellowship (*koinonia*) with our personal God. The true state of being filled with the Holy Spirit includes being sensitive to and understanding that we can have incessant fellowship with Him. We can do nothing without fellowship with the Holy Spirit.

After a few years of being a Christ-follower, I (Dr. Cho) had grown in my faith and discovered that the Holy Spirit is a person. The Scripture helped me understand that He has the characteristics of a person. For example, He can be grieved (Ephesians 4:30; Isaiah 63:10), quenched (1 Thessalonians 5:19), resisted (Acts 7:51), and lied to (Acts 5:3). He intercedes for us (Romans 8:26), and He will communicate with us and lead us into all truth (John 16:13).

Understanding and knowing the characteristics and personality of the Holy Spirit was an epoch-making event that dramatically changed my life. Before that time, I thought of the Holy Spirit as an experience, not as a person. From the time I discovered that the Holy Spirit was a person, I began praying in a personal way. When I went to bed, I said, "Dear Holy Spirit, I sleep now. Tomorrow morning I will see you again." In the morning when I woke up, I prayed, "Dear Holy Spirit, let me serve the Father together with you, in the name of Jesus Christ." Then I went to work. When I preached, I said, "Holy Spirit, I'm going to preach. Work in me with the wisdom, knowledge, and understanding of God."

The Holy Spirit continuously provided me with new dimensions of power, which as a human I could not have imagined. Because I had fellowship with the Holy Spirit, I understood that I must work together with Him. He desires to be our partner. Because the Holy Spirit is the Spirit who works and creates, we should also consult Him about our decisions and behaviors. If we neither acknowledge Him nor welcome Him, even though He is present within us, He cannot work on our behalf. The Holy Spirit is with us and in us (1 Corinthians 3:16; 6:19), and we are one body (12:12–31). Because the Spirit of God lives within us, we cannot act at our own discretion.

The average person makes thirty-five thousand decisions a day. How can we be led by the Holy Spirit and make decisions that will always please God? There are decisions that are obvious: laws we obey, instructions from supervisors, Scriptures that give principles or clear instructions, and areas of common sense. As we listen to Him through our daily decisions, we develop our sensitivity to hearing the voice of the Holy Spirit. In so many areas of our lives, we walk by faith. It is not blind faith, because we have a sense that what we are about to do is in the will of God.

There are disciplines we can apply to our lives that help us become aware of the will of God. These help us understand that what we're about to do is given to us through the Holy Spirit.

Five Steps to Determine the Will of God

Neutral Gear[2]

My (Dr. Cho) first step is to put myself in neutral gear. Not in forward or in reverse, but I endeavor to be completely calm in my heart. Once I'm calm and at peace, then I wait upon the Lord. The Scripture speaks to us about having the "peace of God, which surpasses all understanding" (Philippians 4:7 ESV) and "preaching good news of peace through Jesus Christ" (Acts 10:36 ESV; see also 2 Peter 1:2). Peace is the absence of worry, anxiety, pressure, busyness, or rushing because of a schedule or unnecessary pressure from others.

In our world of social networking, Facebook, texting, the Internet, and cell phones, we must determine not to let these items control our lives or our thinking. Instead, we must control them. To have peace, we need to remove ourselves from a sense of being controlled by the seemingly ongoing pressure of people, technology, and interruptions. When I find the best location, removing the possibility of interruptions, my prayer becomes, "Lord, I am waiting before you, hoping to hear you speak into my spirit. If you say yes, I will go. If you say no, I will not go. I don't wish to make any decisions for my own benefit. I want to decide according to your desire for me. Whether it is good or bad for me, I only want your guidance."

With this attitude, I wait upon the Lord. I've found that many times the best action to take is to fast and pray. Our bodies use energy when we consume large amounts of food. If we eat too much, then we will become so tired that we will not be able to pray. It is only when I know that I have calmed down and put myself in neutral gear where I'm ready to take the second step.

Divine Desire

When I sense that I've calmed my spirit and my mind, I then ask the Lord to reveal His will through my desire. I've found that God always comes to us through our sanctified desires. For example:

Delight yourself in the LORD,
and he will give you the desires of your heart. (Psalm 37:4 ESV)

But the desire of the righteous will be granted. (Proverbs 10:24 ESV)

Therefore I say unto you, What things soever ye desire, when ye pray, believe that ye receive them, and ye shall have them. (Mark 11:24 KJV)

Some feel that desire, in and of itself, is not good. Perhaps they have this opinion because of the environment they grew up in, their education, false religious teaching, or from the idea that all desire is of the flesh. Desires can be from the flesh, and there is no question that we can have wrong desires; however, as we pray and wait upon the Lord, He will give us *His* desires.

I felt the desire to begin a church in a difficult area of Seoul. I desired to give the people hope, healing, and restoration. I sensed a desire to become married to my wife, build our first church building, strategize ways to disciple the people God had entrusted to me, and select certain people to be elders. And each day, I sense desires that I feel are the will of God.

This sensitivity to God's Spirit is developed as we pray and listen to Him. Desire is one of God's focusing points. Philippians tells us, "For it is God who works in you, both to will and to work for his good pleasure" (2:13 ESV). Through the Holy Spirit, God puts His desire in our hearts and the will to do His will. Pray, "Lord, give me the divine desire according to your own will."

As you wait on the Lord through prayer, many desires (beautiful ones) will frequently flow into your mind. When you are praying, have the patience to wait for God's desire to settle in your heart and thinking. Don't stand up and say, "Oh, I've got everything," and rush away. Wait upon the Lord a little longer. Since desires can come from satan, from your own spirit, or from the Holy Spirit, as you wait before the Lord (with an open heart to know His will), one desire will rise above the others. With that desire, you will also sense peace.

One of the ways to sense the Lord's desire is in understanding that the Holy Spirit draws us into the will of God while the devil often pushes and pressures us. If you wait patiently on the Lord, your own desire, or the desires that are from satan, will greatly weaken. The desires from the Holy Spirit, however, will become stronger and stronger. Time is always the test. So wait and receive the divine desire.

Scriptural Screening

When I feel that the right desire from the Holy Spirit has come into clear and sharp focus, that is when I proceed to step three. I then compare the desire I have with what the Bible says. I want to confirm it with Scriptures or with principles that are given in the Word.

One day a lady came to me excited and said, "Oh, Pastor Cho, I am going to support your ministry with a large sum of money."

"Praise God," I said. "Have a seat and tell me about this."

"I have a fantastic desire to go into business," she said as she sat down. "This business is going on, and if I join in, I think I can make big money."

"What kind of business is it?" I asked her.

"I have a burning desire to get a monopoly on the cigarette business." After a slight pause, she added, "Tobacco, you know."

"Forget about it," I said.

"But I have the desire!" she exclaimed. "The burning desire, just like you preached about."

"That desire is from your flesh," I replied. "Have you ever gone through the Bible to see if what you would be doing is scriptural?"

"No," she told me.

"Your desire must be screened through the Scripture," I instructed her. "The Bible says that you are a temple of the Holy Spirit," I went on to explain. "If God ever wanted His people to smoke, then He would have made our noses differently. Smoke stacks are supposed to be open toward the sky, not downward. Think about our noses; they are not pointing up toward the sky but downward. God did not purpose that people should smoke, because our smoke stacks are upside down.

"Your body is the Holy Spirit's dwelling place," I continued. "If you pollute it with smoke, then you are polluting the temple of the Holy Spirit with smoke. Your desire is out of the will of God. It would be best if you just forget about this new business."[3]

On another occasion a man came to me and said, "Pastor, I've struck up a friendship with a beautiful and wonderful woman—a widow. She is sweet, beautiful, and wonderful. And when I pray, I have a burning desire to marry her. But I also have my own wife and children."

"Look," I replied, "you forget about this because it is from the devil."

"Oh, no, no. This is not from the devil," he disagreed. "When I prayed, the Holy Spirit spoke in my heart and told me that my wife was not exactly the right kind of rib to fit into my side. My present wife is always a thorn in my flesh. The Holy Spirit spoke and said that this widow is my lost rib that will fit exactly into my side."

"That is not from the Holy Spirit," I said to him again. "That's from the devil because it's against Scripture." That man did not listen to me; he divorced his wife and married that widow. He is now of all men the most miserable. He found out that his second rib was even worse than his first!

When I (Wayde) was a young Christian (twenty-one years old), a well-known pastor came to minister at the mission church I attended on Guam. He was greatly used of God and spoke with anointed authority. People were healed and delivered from bondage through his ministry. As a new Christian, I was greatly impressed with his communication skills and the ways God used him.

A short time after that visiting pastor went back to his home church, I asked the missionary for an update: "How is that pastor doing? Are you going to invite him back to our church?"

The missionary said that he had been concerned that if he told me what was going on, I might stumble in my faith. He then went on to say, "After his meetings at our church, that pastor returned to his church and informed them that he felt that the will of God was for him to leave his wife and four young children and marry another woman, with whom he was having an affair."

I was shocked. Even though I was new Christian, I knew this was not the will of God. It was a demonically inspired, foolish desire of that pastor's flesh, which the man had rationalized as the will of God. He was absolutely wrong. Many people make this kind of mistake when discerning their desires. Our fleshly desires, as well as demonic desires, tend to fade away as we pray within the parameters of the written Word of God.

The Holy Spirit will never contradict the written Word. All our desires should be carefully screened with the Scriptures. If you don't have the knowledge or self-confidence to do this yourself, then go to a godly, wise Christian and ask him or her to help you to discern where your desires come from. Your pastor, small group or cell leader, or accountability group of friends who are wise in their faith and in the Scriptures can pray and counsel you. Discuss with them the desire you have or the plans you're making, asking them for advice, wisdom, and prayer as you endeavor to walk in the will of God.

A Beckoning Signal

After I screen my desire through God's written Word, then I'm ready for step four: I simply ask God for a beckoning signal from my circumstances. If God has truly spoken to your heart, then He will certainly give you a signal from the external world. A situation or circumstance will become apparent to you, thus confirming God's will for your life.

When Elijah prayed seven times for rain, he received a signal from the eastern sky. A cloud as large as a man's fist appeared (1 Kings 18:44–46). Gideon also asked for a sign from God and received one—twice (Judges 6:11–40). In the New Testament, Paul had a vision to go to Macedonia (Acts 16:6–10). The Bible gives us numerous examples about how God provided a "signal or sign" to a person as he or she sought to walk in His will.

In all my years of ministry, God has shown me signs in my different circumstances. Sometimes the signs are huge, but at other times they're small. As you determine to hear the voice of the Holy Spirit regarding His will, you'll develop more sensitivity and awareness of His signs through divine circumstances.

Divine Timing

After I receive a sign or sense the will of God, then I move on to the final stage. I pray and wait until I have peace that I'm on target with God's timing. If you still feel restless in your spirit regarding your desire, that means the timing isn't right. There's still a red light, so keep praying and waiting. When you see the green light, peace will come into your heart and you'll know it is time to go.

It is important to remember that our timing is not God's timing. He is all-knowing and understands what needs to happen for doors to open. Perhaps there are people He will remove from the situation, or people who still need to change their minds, for certain doors to open. God knows the future and the exact season, day, or hour when we need to move forward by faith.

When you sense the peace of God, along with the divine desire to do what is in your heart, you should jump up and go with full speed. When you go with God's blessing in accordance with His Word, miracle after miracle will follow you. All my Christian life I have developed and conducted my ministry using these five simple steps, and God has confirmed His will with signs and miracles along the way.

Mountain-Moving Faith

There is always a significant element of faith involved when walking in the will of God. Jesus says that we should have faith in God, for then we will be able to move mountains: "Have faith in God. Truly, I say to you, whoever says to this mountain, 'Be taken up and thrown into the sea,' and does not doubt in his heart, but believes that what he says will come to pass, it will be done for him" (Mark 11:22–23 ESV).

When we receive the Word of God, we have received faith from God. The faith did not come from you; it is imparted faith that God has given to you. After receiving this imparted faith, you can command the mountains of impossibilities, hindrances, and obstacles to be removed. Impossible situations, illnesses, family dysfunctions, and tragic experiences that have bound people can be removed in the name of Jesus. But without receiving God's faith, we cannot do this.

The Scriptures are God's written Word. It's critical that we discipline ourselves to consistently read, study, and pray the Word. In 2 Timothy 3:16, we read that God "breathed" the Scriptures out, which means He inspired them and imparted life into them. His Word has supernatural power, gives us specific instructions, and will speak to our mind and our spirit. This wonderful gift tells us how to live a life that will glorify Him, be successful, and lead to eternal life with our Lord and Savior.

We should carefully study the Bible, from Genesis through Revelation, in order to give the Holy Spirit the material in our hearts that He wants to work with. Then, when you wait upon the Lord, the Holy Spirit will impart faith to you. And great miracles will follow as you step out in faith—miracles in your family, personal life, career, and ministry.

Wait on the Lord. Never consider it a waste of time. When God speaks to your heart, He can do far greater in a moment than you could do in years of struggle. Be patient and wait upon the Lord, for you will see great things.

4

The Principles of Faith

The prayer of a righteous person
is powerful and effective.
—James 5:16

Many have called Yoido Full Gospel Church a miracle; we're told that it is the largest church in the world. I (Dr. Cho), too, believe it is a miracle; however, I don't want anyone to be misled: we have many thousands of wonderful workers who are deeply committed, spiritually gifted, and hardworking in their service to our people.

We also do not want to give the impression that every church can or should be like the Yoido church in its size or influence. South Korea is a unique culture that has been deeply impacted by the Korean War and the threat from the north. We continue to pray for peace; however, we are aware of potential challenges that could come. This tension is to our advantage as many have developed their prayer lives, their faith, and their commitment to Christ.

Experience Builds Faith

So many miracles begin with small beginnings. When I began this ministry, we held services in a small tent. I felt impressed to go to a section of Seoul that was in great need, a community of poor, destitute, and hopeless people. City slum dwellers desperately needed something to believe in, a message that would give them hope. If I could preach and teach God's truths about salvation in Jesus Christ and give them hope for their lives, then I knew it would be of great help. I explained that God desires to be a friend to the people and that He will give them many blessings as they depend on and trust in Him.

From the beginning, we believed in miracles, signs, and wonders, and the necessity of being baptized in the Holy Spirit. Throughout the years (which has now been six decades!), I've seen Christ heal countless people. They're healed of many kinds of diseases, emotional torments, demon possession, and addictions. Over the years, as I have watched people change before my eyes because of their faith in Christ, they go and tell their friends, relatives, and others in the community about the power of God.

I am not ashamed of the gospel,
for it is the power of God for salvation
for everyone who believes.
—Romans 12:1 ESV

I felt that if I could offer people hope—a way to get out of their desperation and believe in the power of the gospel—then that would be part of the solution. I have believed for thousands of people, prayed for the sick, and found ways to help with peoples' physical needs. And God has provided wonderful miracles.

In the beginning, I believed and dreamed for less than I do today. Back then, I thought the dream that God had given me was huge, but today I believe for so much more. My experience in Christ and my trust in Him has grown and built my faith as I have been a personal witness of His miracles. As you take steps of faith, trust God's Word, and hear His voice, then you too will grow as God honors your decision and answers your prayer.

Faith Is Contagious—So Is Fear

"Without faith it is impossible to please God, because anyone who comes to him must believe that he exists and that he rewards those who earnestly seek him" (Hebrews 11:6). We grow as we step out by faith and experience God's power. Seeing that what we believed for happened gives us courage to believe for even more.

This is a principle the early disciples learned from Jesus. They were with Him when many miracles happened, and those experiences encouraged them to believe. They, too, went out among the people and miracles occurred. People were healed, the demon-possessed were set free, and lives were miraculously changed. These early disciples observed what Jesus did when miracles happened, they were instructed to do what He did, and, as a result, God honored their faith.

Because we believe for something we don't yet see with our eyes, there is always risk with faith. The apostles and many followers of Jesus had watched and been with Jesus for approximately three years, and they saw the resurrected Jesus and had been told that they had authority over unclean spirits, to cast them out, and to heal every disease and every affliction (Matthew 10:1; Luke 9:1; 10:19). They took the risk of believing and trusting by faith, and their faith worked.

This brings tremendous opportunities and amazing information about who God is and what He can do through our lives when we're submitted to Him. Paul had this in mind in 1 Corinthians 2:9–10 (ESV): "'What no eye has seen, nor ear heard nor the heart of man imagined, what God has prepared for those who love him'—these things God has revealed to us through the Spirit. For the Spirit searches everything, even the depths of God."

Throughout the years, there are many principles I've learned about how to grow in my personal faith, as well as how to help others grow in theirs. Faith is contagious, so it's important that we have relationships with people of faith and are part of a church whose leaders believe that God is an ever-present God who can perform miracles. Faith doesn't grow naturally, but we must continue to be hungry and sincere in our desire to be stronger in our trust in God and have faith in what He can do.[1]

Here are a few principles of faith we have applied to our lives; they have greatly impacted us.

The Holy Spirit Continually Helps Us as We Walk by Faith

Much of what we do is greatly influenced by our physical senses—hearing, seeing, smelling, tasting, and touching. We tend to learn from our experiences, the environment around us, cultures we grow up in, and other people we encounter. Depending on our education, we most often acquire information that is rational and can be proven experimentally. However, there is knowledge that is not based on our personal knowledge or senses—it surpasses the rationale or wisdom of humans. It is revelation knowledge.

Revelation knowledge is acquired by the work of the Holy Spirit, who is actively involved in our lives. He will bring us truths that we could not learn with our basic senses. Paul reminded the Corinthians of this when he wrote: "We have received not the spirit of the world, but the Spirit who is from God, that we might understand the things freely given us by God. And we impart this in words not taught by human wisdom but taught by the Spirit, interpreting spiritual truths to those who are spiritual" (1 Corinthians 2:12–13 ESV).

The Holy Spirit always reveals wonderful truths as we study and meditate on the Word of God, taking time to listen to His voice.

Paul wanted others to understand that he didn't minister from his own human abilities or knowledge that was acquired from his secular or well-respected religious education. He also faced physical and emotional challenges—possibly the fear of public speaking or other anxieties about the group he was addressing. He wanted the Christians in Corinth to understand that he didn't depend on his human abilities, but instead he trusted in God's supernatural power when he ministered to them. He explained: "And I was with you in weakness and in fear and much trembling, and my speech and my message were not in plausible words of wisdom, but in demonstration of the Spirit and of power, that your faith might not rest in the wisdom of men but in the power of God" (1 Corinthians 2:3–5 ESV).

It's critical that we know who the Holy Spirit is because, as Christ-followers, He lives within us. From the moment you accept Jesus into your life, the Holy Spirit makes His dwelling in you. He invades your life and you become His temple (1 Corinthians 3:16; 6:19). Because you're a temple of the Holy Spirit, you have unique sensitivities that you didn't have before becoming a Christian.

The Holy Spirit can be hurt and grieved by our sinful behavior, harmful words, and negative and critical attitudes, as Paul tells us in Ephesians 4:30 (ESV): "And do not grieve the Holy Spirit of God, with whom you were sealed for the day of redemption." He's the truth teller and helps us sense when we're going in the wrong direction. He will help us understand how to mature and become wiser. As believers, when we feel conviction in our lives concerning some activity, attitude, or sinful thinking, this is the Holy Spirit helping us. We may begin feeling uncomfortable, or start questioning something that we are thinking or are about to do, which helps us turn from our behavior or doubt. We can then choose to repent and draw near to God.

The Holy Spirit helps us recognize that we're without hope unless we receive Jesus Christ as Lord and Savior. Paul writes, "No one can say, 'Jesus is Lord' except in the Holy Spirit" (1 Corinthians 12:3 ESV). The Holy Spirit guides us into truth and will remind us of all that Jesus promised, even about the future (John 16:12–15). Our faith in God is strengthened and renewed when the Holy Spirit reveals to us His truth.

From the moment you accept Jesus into your life, you are "marked with a seal of the promised Holy Spirit" (Ephesians 1:13 ESV). It's the Holy Spirit who gives you the assurance that you're born again in Christ and that you are indeed a child of God (John 1:12). Not only that, but Scripture tells us so much about the Holy Spirit. Here is just some of what it says:

- He is our Helper who will always be with us (John 14:16; 16:7).
- He reveals to us the truth about Jesus (14:17, 26).
- He informs us of truth and will guide us into truth (14:17, 26; 16:13).
- He dwells in us and will speak to us (14:17; 16:13).
- He will help us bring glory to Jesus (16:14).
- He will tell us about the future (16:13).
- He convicts us of our guilt (16:7–8).
- He gives us the new birth (3:3–6).
- He fuses (incorporates) us into the body of Christ (1 Corinthians 12:13).
- With our salvation we receive the Spirit (John 3:36; 20:22), and, as a result, we become participants in the divine nature (2 Peter 1:4).
- We can be "baptized with the Holy Spirit," resulting in greater power to be witnesses for Jesus (Acts 1:5, 8; 2:4, 38–39; Luke 24:39).

The Scripture is God's revelation, and the Spirit of God gives us understanding and knowledge about how to apply the truths of the Scripture. People of the world frequently mock God because they do not (cannot) understand the Bible. Without the illumination of the

Holy Spirit, the human mind cannot understand the Bible. It is the Holy Spirit who gives revelation knowledge and encourages faith.

Oh, this baptism of the Holy Spirit is an inward presence
of the personality of God, which lifts, prays, takes hold,
lives in with a tranquility of peace and power that
rests and says, "It is all right." God answers prayer
because the Holy Spirit prays and your advocate is Jesus,
and the Father the Judge of all. There He is.
Is it possible for any prayer to be missed on those lines?

—Smith Wigglesworth, *Smith Wigglesworth on Prayer*

When we become a child of God, our natural "measure of faith" begins to supernaturally grow. As we read and meditate on God's Word, He will illuminate the truths of the Bible and personally speak to us through the Scripture. The Holy Spirit is fully God and is our wonderful Helper, Counselor, and Comforter. He desires and deserves a personal, intimate relationship. A well-balanced Christian life is only possible through our close fellowship with the Holy Spirit.

If we think of the Holy Spirit as a theological "object" and refer to Him as "it," then we do not understand His work and ministry as we should. The Holy Spirit has an intellect, emotions, and a will—all the attributes of personality. He is the third person of the Trinity, one on whom we can depend for counsel, comfort, and conviction. If we do this, our fellowship with Him will continually grow and we'll become stronger in our faith.

Effective Prayer Grows Our Faith

We all know that if we stop breathing for several minutes, we will die. Faith can be compared to breathing: It's essential for our survival. To possess a vibrant faith, we need to pray earnestly, for prayer will give us strength and the ability to hear from our Creator. He will give us the answers we need and the fulfillment of our dreams. Just as we should breathe air regularly to survive, so we need to pray to live a victorious life.

It's important to set aside special time to be alone with God in prayer. Many people have heard of the strong faith of the Korean Christians. If this is the case, it's only because of their morning prayers. A high percentage of us get up early each morning to read the Bible and pray. And most of us pray for more than an hour each morning. If you pray at least one hour every morning, then your faith will never be weak; it will only become stronger and stronger.

Our faith is activated and grows in our daily lives largely because of our determination to understand God's Word, to pray, and to listen to the Holy Spirit. Many Christians have an immature prayer life that consists of just asking or begging for something. Please understand that the Lord wants us to ask Him (pray) for our needs; however, if this is all we do, then we don't understand the vastness and the wonderful blessings that come as we communicate with and listen to the Holy Spirit.

The Bible gives us hundreds of examples of ways to pray or to offer prayers. Just one example is when Paul encouraged Timothy, "I urge that supplications, prayers, intercessions, and thanksgivings be made for all people" (1 Timothy 2:1 ESV). In the Yoido Full Gospel Church, we observe many kinds of prayer: we pray quietly, pray in unison, pray as a congregation, have times of fasting and prayer, and have morning prayer and all-night prayer meetings. I often write my prayers and read them to God.

Great triumphs can only come out of great trials.
—Smith Wigglesworth

For those who have had a disciplined prayer life, it's not uncommon for them to be able to pray quietly or even silently. Frequently there are distractions and difficulties that influence their thoughts; however, they've grown to a point where they can listen to the Lord and pray silently despite what is going on around them.

For young believers, unison prayer with others is more beneficial. They can hear what another person prays for, and the sound of others praying will encourage them to learn to pray more fervently. Praying together is a tremendous opportunity for you to communicate with your Creator and see Him answer. By praying with all our heart, we will surely touch the throne of God and our faith will be activated. Jesus promised us, "Truly, truly, I say to you, whatever you ask of the Father in my name, he will give it to you" (John 16:23 ESV).

We Trust the Scriptures

Many ask why we need to grow in our faith in the first place. As new Christians, we become aware of how the Bible makes sense and how it speaks to our lives. The Scripture tells us, "Like newborn infants, long for the pure spiritual milk, that by it you may grow up into salvation—if indeed you have tasted that the Lord is good" (1 Peter 2:2–3 ESV). We need the nourishment from the Scriptures. When we're young in our faith, or "newborn," and hear the Scriptures being taught and read, it will feed our spirit and strengthen our faith. "Pure spiritual milk" is a symbol of our basic need to grow as Christians.

As new Christians, we will only grow as much as we read, apply, and obey God's Word. Our faith largely depends on our discipline to understand Scripture and let it speak into our lives. There are many Christians who have known the Lord for years but are still babies in the faith. They don't understand the deeper truths of the Word, nor do they have discernment that Scripture teaches us about. The letter to the Hebrews address this issue:

> For though by this time you ought to be teachers, you need someone to teach you again the basic principles of the oracles of God. You need milk, not solid food, for everyone who lives on milk is unskilled in the word of righteousness, since he is a child. But solid food is for the mature, for those who have their powers of discernment trained by constant practice to distinguish good from evil.
>
> Therefore let us leave the elementary doctrine of Christ and go on to maturity .... (Hebrews 5:12–6:1 ESV)

We're born with unique personalities; however, we can grow in our character and mature in our faith. Character is developed as we mature in our faith. Peter gives us many qualities that the Holy Spirit will help us add to our maturing faith. He writes:

> His divine power has given us everything we need for a godly life through our knowledge of him who called us by his own glory and goodness. Through these he has given us his very great and precious promises, so that through them you may participate in the divine nature, having escaped the corruption in the world caused by evil desires.
>
> For this very reason, make every effort to add to your faith goodness; and to goodness, knowledge; and to knowledge, self-control; and to self-control, perseverance; and to perseverance, godliness; and to godliness, mutual affection; and to mutual affection, love. For if you possess these qualities in increasing measure, they will keep you from being ineffective and unproductive in your knowledge of our Lord Jesus Christ. But whoever does not have them

is nearsighted and blind, forgetting that they have been cleansed from their past sins.

Therefore, my brothers and sisters, make every effort to confirm your calling and election. For if you do these things, you will never stumble, and you will receive a rich welcome into the eternal kingdom of our Lord and Savior Jesus Christ. (2 Peter 1:3–11)

The Word is powerful and full of God's promises. It gives us many examples of people who walked by faith, repented of their sins, and turned back to wholeheartedly follow God, and those who acted inappropriately and sinned. Examples are given about how to live a successful life and how to be forgiven and restored if we've failed. We desperately need the Word of God to teach us the marvelous truths about our salvation, as well as increase our understanding of the mysteries of God.

We should pray with the psalmist, "Your word is a lamp to my feet, a light on my path" (Psalm 119:105).

Using Our Words in the Right Way

Our faith is strengthened, or weakened, by the words we use and the thoughts we permit to occupy our minds. What we say to ourselves, what we permit ourselves to think about, and what we believe about our potential can either help us or hurt us. So many people continually use negative, doubtful, and harmful words when they speak of themselves. They make statements like:

- "I can't do it."
- "I'm not good enough."
- "I'm not very intelligent."
- "I could never be the person I would like to be."

Why do so many people use these kinds of statements when they are speaking of themselves? It is no wonder that many struggle with self-confidence. Your tongue can say words that make you either weaker or stronger, confident or lacking confidence, secure or insecure. James has much to say about the power of our words:

> For we all stumble in many ways. And if anyone does not stumble in what he says, he is a perfect man, able to bridle his whole body. If we put bits into the mouths of horses so that they obey us, we guide their whole bodies as well. Look at the ships also: though they are so large and are driven by strong winds, they are guided by a very small rudder wherever the will of the pilot directs. So also the tongue is a small member, yet it boasts of great things.
>
> How great a forest is set ablaze by such a small fire! (James 3:2–5 ESV)

God has promised you an abundant life (John 10:10); you're a child of God (John 1:12). You've been forgiven (1 John 1:9) and are qualified to share in the inheritance of the saints in light (Colossians 1:12). You've been delivered from the domain of darkness and are now in God's kingdom (Colossians 1:13). You've been redeemed (Colossians 1:14), you're a temple of the Holy Spirit (1 Corinthians 6:19), and you have the mind of Christ (1 Corinthians 2:16). God has a plan for your future (Jeremiah 29:11).

You must continue to remind yourself (and others) of who you are as a child of God and speak words of faith, trust, and victory. If you don't know who you are, then other people will tell you who you are. God tells you who you are in His Word. You know who you are by knowing *whose* you are.

There is surely a future hope for you,
and your hope will not be cut off.
—Proverbs 23:18

When Abraham was a hundred years old and Sarah was ninety, God put a bit in their mouths, causing them by faith to speak as Abraham and Sarah, the "father of many nations" (Genesis 17:4–5; Romans 4:17–18) and the "mother of nations" (Genesis 17:16). Although they couldn't physically see themselves in this way, they believed and acknowledged this revelation from God. By faith they recognized and called each other these new names, and because of God's promise they became the father and mother of all nations!

We make it hard for our Christian faith to grow when we speak negatively. Saying such things as "I can't do this" or "I'm not good at anything" can injure our faith. We've often heard people say, "This can't be done" or "We've tried this before and it didn't work." These are faith-killing statements. If our words are full of complaint, gossip, slander, and negativity, then we need to seek God's help to turn us in a positive direction.

Satan will certainly attack us and endeavor to bring doubt, negative or harmful words, and words of accusation to our minds. He desires a foothold to trap us and destroy our faith. Without thinking, we can open ourselves up to his attacks and to the forces of darkness. The enemy loves it when we use inappropriate words and words of doubt and unbelief. He understands that when we trust God, pray in belief, and have faith that He will do what He promised, there is tremendous power.

Proverbs tells us, "Death and life are in the power of the tongue, and those who love it will eat its fruit" (Proverbs 18:21 ESV). With God's help, we can discipline our conversations and prayers. We can make a conscious effort to speak helpful and good words— words of life and encouragement. We can also quote the promises found in the Scriptures and develop a stronger faith. Paul reminds us to dwell on positive things by writing, "Finally, brothers and sisters, whatever is true, whatever is noble, whatever is right, whatever is pure, whatever is lovely, whatever is admirable—if anything is excellent or praiseworthy—think about such things" (Philippians 4:8 ESV).

Our Faith Will Always Be Tested

When God called Abraham to leave his home and follow Him, he obeyed God's divine command without fully understanding the way of faith. The Lord told Abraham that He would make him into a great nation, and through him all the families of the earth would be blessed (Genesis 12:1-4). Abraham certainly didn't fully understand what this meant, but he made the decision to believe and trust God.

When he was seventy-five, Abraham received the promise that God would give him a son. However, Sarah and Abraham doubted God's promise because for years they tried but did not have a child. So they decided to take matters into their own hands, and Abraham committed a sinful act with Sarah's servant Hagar. As a result, Hagar became pregnant with Ishmael. This decision caused insurmountable challenges for thousands of years. Abraham recognized what he did and came back to what God had promised (Genesis 15:5-6; Romans 4:18-22).

Our faith will always be tested. Another incredible test came to Abraham later when God asked him to sacrifice his promised son Isaac as a burnt offering. Abraham learned to trust and to have faith. He believed that if God asked him to do this, then He would provide another sacrifice or raise his son from the dead (Genesis 17:8, 12; Hebrews 11:17-19). He had glorious faith when he obeyed God.

To live by faith, we must have a loving relationship with our Father God (John 1:12). When we receive Jesus Christ as our Savior, we grow in our understanding that He deeply loves us (John 3:16). Understanding this love, we tend to make decisions to obey God, grow in our knowledge of His Word, and live by faith

(Romans 10:17). We follow the navigation of the Holy Spirit who is our Counselor, Helper, and Comforter (John 14:16–18, 26; 16:13), for He will tell us when to go to the right or to the left. That is why we need to obey Him and stand on His Word.

Remember that there's a fight between our faith and our senses. The devil often attacks us through our senses; therefore, we must clearly understand the Word of God (John 1:1; Hebrews 11:3), accepting it deep into our hearts. Let us make a firm decision to believe in the Word of God without compromise and without looking back (see Luke 9:62; Hebrews 10:38). Let us make a proclamation of faith, which is like a sword that attacks the devil.

The way of faith can be difficult at times. But if you start by faith and then stumbled or fell because you relied on your natural senses, then stand up once again. Love, serve, and obey God. Stand on His Word. Make a proclamation of faith today. Endeavor to live by faith, not by sight, and God will perform miracles in your life.

5

What Weakens Our Faith?

I pray, and I obey.

—Yonggi Cho

One day, during a church service, a man started running back and forth across the back of the sanctuary as the pastor was preaching. Obviously, the congregation seemed distracted, but the pastor didn't stop him. A friend and I (Dr. Cho) were there to minister, and since we were not familiar with the style of the services, we wondered if this was a common practice. Soon the man started running around the sanctuary again but then finally sat down for the remainder of the church service.

As we were leaving, I turned to the pastor and asked about the running man. "Why was he running around the sanctuary during the message?"

"I don't know," the pastor said. "But he hasn't been able to walk for over ten years."

Something happened to that man during the time of worship and during the message. His faith was supercharged, and he began to believe. There was no doubt that the presence of the Lord was there, as He is "always there" when two or more are gathered in His name (Matthew 18:20). The man was stirred in his spirit to the point that he stood up and walked—even ran. Even though I can't explain this, on many occasions I have witnessed these kinds of miracles.

Before I was a Christ-follower and was terminally ill, the young girl who witnessed to me and gave me her Bible told me to read the book of Matthew. Even as an unbeliever, when reading Matthew 8–9, I thought Jesus was a doctor. I was right, as He is our Divine Physician. The Word tells us that Jesus "bore our sins in His own body on the tree, that we, having died to sins, might live for righteousness—by whose stripes you were healed" (1 Peter 2:24 NKJV).

When people hear the truths of the Scripture, and their hearts are open to the Holy Spirit, miracles frequently happen. There are numerous examples of and references to healing throughout the Scriptures. Faith is an obvious ingredient for physical, emotional, relational, and spiritual healing. Jesus said, "For assuredly, I say to you, whoever says to this mountain, 'Be removed and be cast into the sea,' and does not doubt in his heart, but believes that those things he says will come to pass, he will have whatever he says" (Mark 11:23–24 NKJV).

At times, faith seems to come from the person who is doing the praying. At other times, however, the individual senses or believes that healing is happening and then makes the decision to believe. On many occasions, we've prayed for a person and healing has occurred, or we have observed a person or group of people receive healing during a time of worship and/or teaching of the Word. But there have been other times when people are not healed. During those times, we must remind ourselves that we're not the healer—God is. There could be reasons why the person isn't healed in that moment. The absence of healing when praying for someone should not inhibit us from praying, however. We must pray the prayer of faith and trust God with the results.

Having faith when we pray is critical. We know that "nothing is impossible with God" (Luke 1:37 NLT). He asks us to pray in faith, believing that He hears and responds to our prayers. At times, His response is immediate, while at other times He waits for the person or situation to develop. During all these times we continue to pray, believing He is the God of miracles.

Daniel prayed for twenty-one days but did not receive a response to his request (Daniel 10:12–13). However, when Daniel began praying, God immediately responded and sent the answer, but an evil angel (demon) prevented God's messenger from bringing the response to Daniel. We should note that this particular spiritual opponent was powerful and had the ability to delay God's messenger for three weeks. But remember, all he could do was delay the answer. God responded by sending Michael, the archangel, to help God's messenger so he could bring the answer to Daniel.

The enemy will do everything he can to prevent answers to prayer from getting to us. During those times, we keep believing, keep praying, and keep having faith. God always hears the prayers of the righteous and will respond appropriately.

Doubt Weakens Our Faith

The opposite of faith is doubt. For many, this doubt could come in the form of fear, unbelief, or believing that signs, wonders, and miracles don't happen today. Some have overthought and overanalyzed the topic of faith and have come to a conclusion that the tremendous influence of the Holy Spirit and the miracles we read about in the book of Acts discontinued when the early apostles died. If you are full of doubt or unbelief, then we want to challenge you to begin taking small steps of faith.

There are many steps we can take to strengthen our faith; there are also many steps we can take to increase our doubt. Remember that "faith is confidence in what we hope for and assurance about what we do not see" (Hebrews 11:1).

The Bible tells us that one of the purposes of trials in our lives is to test our faith. James instructs us to bring our request for wisdom to God through prayer, expecting an answer. He also explains what doubt does to us as we try to pray with faith:

> Consider it pure joy, my brothers and sisters, whenever you face trials of many kinds, because you know that the testing of your faith produces perseverance. Let perseverance finish its work so that you may be mature and complete, not lacking anything. If any of you lacks wisdom, you should ask God, who gives generously to all without finding fault and it will be given to you. But when you ask, you must believe and not doubt, because the one who doubts is like a wave of the sea, blown and tossed by the wind. That person should not expect to receive anything from the Lord. Such a person is double-minded and unstable in all they do. (James 1:2–8)

We made the decision to believe that Jesus Christ is Lord and that He physically rose from the dead by faith. Because of that, we were saved (Romans 10:9–10). Faith (belief) is always needed because it's required with our salvation.

After we accept Christ, we're to continue living by faith. Some take great steps of faith while others take smaller steps, while still others waver in their faith and are indecisive, going back and forth between believing and doubting; they are up one moment and down the next. In fact, they can't make up their minds. They're "double-minded."

I'm trying here to prevent anyone saying the really foolish thing that people often say about Him: 'I'm ready to accept Jesus as a great moral teacher, but I don't accept His claim to be God.' That is the one thing we must not say. A man who was merely a man and said the sort of things Jesus said would not be a great moral teacher. He would either be a lunatic—on the level with a man who says he is a poached egg—or else he would be the Devil of Hell. You must make your choice. Either this man was, and is, the Son of God: or else a madman or something worse.

—C. S. Lewis, *Mere Christianity*

Double-minded people go back and forth in their thinking. One moment they might have strong confidence in God, perhaps because they heard a tremendous message where their faith was encouraged, but later, when they get back to their normal daily lives, they become full of doubt once again. Worry and fear creep in, and perhaps they even imagine their lives are falling apart. Doubt and fear have become stronger than faith.

Genuine faith is the confident confession that God will do what He has promised. The danger comes when we take our eyes off Him, begin looking at circumstances, or believe the doubts or criticism of others. Maybe we begin to listen to the voice of the enemy, the devil, who does not want us to grow in our confidence in God. When we take our eyes off God and His promises, our faith can change to doubt and our confidence in His ability to help us can change to anxiety and worry.

James tells us that when we start doubting, then we're driven and tossed around like waves in the ocean (James 1:6). He explains that when people are double-minded, they are unstable (v. 8). Because of this instability, they really should not expect anything from the Lord. Their prayers may go unanswered and they may not receive what they want because they doubt God. Their prayer is only words, and without faith their words are empty. With faith, our prayers are powerful.

All of us have times when we feel tested in our faith. During these times, we need to examine the promises of God in the Scriptures and believe. No matter how we feel or what others (who are full of doubt and cynicism) are telling us, we make the decision to have faith. Don't be mistaken—all Christians go through times when we feel like we're standing alone on the personal promises God has given us.

Having questions about something we're praying about is not necessarily the same as having doubt. When we question something, we are only seeking more information. We desire greater understanding that will help us ensure that we're accurately hearing from the Lord. During those times, we study the Word, endeavoring to be certain that our opinion or act of faith has scriptural support. When we doubt, on the other hand, we make the decision to believe what we think, see, or feel rather than what God has said. It's normal to question when we're suddenly overwhelmed by a crisis, tragedy, or an attack from the enemy (or from people the enemy is using).

God is a miraculous God, and throughout history He has moved in powerful ways. The Bible is a living book that is "God-breathed" (2 Timothy 3:16). In it, He gives us numerous examples of people who had great faith. When we read about those "witnesses" who have lived before us (Hebrews 12:1), we sense that God can use us in similar ways. He desires us to understand that He has always performed miracles and answered prayers for His children.

There have been times in our lives where the situation did not look optimistic because we were being attacked by misinformation, slander, gossip, half-truths, and untruths. During those times, it can be easy to permit our minds to doubt the deliverance that God will bring. Our Lord certainly understands the struggles we go through and desires that we come to Him when we're facing an attack, confusion, pain, illness, or any other kind of need. He will be our defender (if we permit Him) and give us peace during the storm.

Instead of spending our time worrying or suffering with anxiety, we can make the decision to find a place of solitude and pray. The psalmist invites us to cast our cares on the Lord: "Cast your cares on the LORD and he will sustain you; he will never let the righteous be shaken" (Psalm 55:22). In prayer, we give our worries to the Lord, and then listen to the gentle voice of the Holy Spirit. He will often speak to us as we meditate on the promises of God contained in His Scriptures. Then we're able to evaluate what we're going through and compare it to the promises God has given us.

At times, God shifts our thinking and reminds us of His truth, and how He has been faithful to us in the past. He brings to mind the times He has been with us when we've gone through a testing of our faith or a crisis, or when we have needed to be restored from mistakes or sin. If we look back, we can see God's faithfulness, His answers to prayer, and the many occasions when He supernaturally intervened in our lives.

Sometimes people ask, "How can I know the will of God and when He is talking to me?" Much of the time we know the will of God by looking backward. When we look back, we see how God helped us and walked with us through trials and difficult decisions. We have faith about the future because He has been faithful to us in the past. You are His child; He will not change His mind about His promises for you.

Why Do We Doubt?

There are many reasons why we doubt. Even after we have known the Lord for many years, there will still be challenges and heartaches, along with spiritual, emotional, physical, and relational situations that can challenge our faith. During these times, it is possible to doubt. Here are some common ways that doubt enters into our lives.

We're Involved in a Challenge That Seems Abnormal

One common reason that doubt enters our lives is that we're involved in circumstances that go against human reasoning. When Peter saw Jesus walking on water, he said, "Lord, if it's you … tell me to come to you on the water." The Lord said, "Come," and Peter began to walk on the water (Matthew 14:28–29)—at least for a few steps. Peter stepped on the water with confidence, but as soon as he took his eyes off Jesus and focused the wind and waves, he began to sink. He started out thinking, *By faith I can do this.* But when he looked away from Jesus, he probably started thinking, *People can't walk on water,* and his faith faltered.

We're much like Peter when we add human reasoning to God's promises or commands. Instead of believing, we often doubt. For example:

- Concerning forgiveness, our logic may ask us, *Why should I forgive someone who has brought great harm to my family or me?*
- Concerning observing the Sabbath, our logic might say, *Why would I give one day a week to do nothing except rest, relax, and refresh myself when I could use that extra day to get caught up with work?*
- Concerning our obedience in tithing to God's work, our logic asks, *How can a person live off 90 percent more successfully than 100 percent of their income? Giving 10 percent doesn't make sense.*
- Concerning returning harm or defending ourselves, our logic asks, *Why should I bless those who curse me, pray*

*for those who mistreat me, and turn my other cheek when
someone hits me (Luke 6:28)?*

Giving forgiveness, observing the Sabbath, tithing, and not returning harm when we've been harmed are just some of the principles that
can go against our human reasoning. However, these few examples
(and hundreds of others) are God's truths we can depend on.

"Give, and will be given to you."

—Luke 6:38

We Allow Our Feelings to Overcome Our Faith

We can always be confident that if the Lord asks us to do something, then He will give us the ability to do it. Even when we're
tempted to do something sinful, the Bible says that God will provide a way out (1 Corinthians 10:13). If we permit fear or a sense of
inadequacy or unworthiness to cause us to doubt His promises, we
can miss opportunities because of our disobedience. When tempted
to do or say something wrong or sinful, we can take God's way, or
do what we're temped to do and become snared by the enemy.

Because the Holy Spirit lives within us, we can live a supernatural life in His power—that is, if we choose to obey Him. We're called
to live by faith, not fear.

We Can't See God in What Is Happening to Us

The Lord has promised to take care of us, but it might not be
in the way we expect or want at the time. We may think that the
Lord couldn't possibly be in the midst of our difficult or painful
situation, but the truth is that He is. According to Romans 8:28, "in
all things God works for the good of those who love him, who have
been called according to his purpose."

Many times we have made the decision to trust God and wait on His timing. Even during times of confusion, He can be trusted. He will not abandon or ignore us, but He will be there in these complicated times and work for our good. He will vindicate us when the time is right—we can rest in the fact that He is working on our behalf.

When your life situation seems like a "perfect storm" has hit you, you can do the right thing, trust God, permit Him to be your defender, and keep your focus on Jesus.

We Listen to People's Voices of Doubt

When we're trying to discern the will of God, we must be careful who we ask for advice. Some friends are helpful as they offer wise counsel and pray with us as we seek the Lord's direction. Their words are encouraging, truthful, and wise. However, others might tell us what they would do in that situation or even just say what they think we want to hear. Their response may be commonsense advice at best (which is not always wrong), but can lack faith and spiritual wisdom. There are others who think they are giving wise advice by informing us that our hopes are not practical or reasonable. They cause us to question God's promises versus trusting His Word.

We need to be cautious about whom we listen to and whom we associate with. Proverbs reminds us, "Walk with the wise and become wise, for a companion of fools suffers harm" (Proverbs 13:20).

We Can Only See the Problem, Not the Solution

Another thing that weakens faith and increases doubt is that we can't get our minds off the negative circumstance in our lives. In fact, little problems become large when they preoccupy our thinking. This is why we must always consider every situation that we go through in the light of our great God and His promises. He can handle anything and everything we experience. Worry, anxiety, and fretting demonstrate that we do not trust the Lord. Our thinking determines our behavior; we can discipline ourselves to think on God's promises, blessings, favor, and His love for us. God said through Jeremiah, "For I know the plans I have for you, declares the LORD, plans for welfare and not for evil, to give you a future and a hope" (Jeremiah 29:11 ESV).

We Question the Way God Is Working

Another reason we often doubt is because we may not have the full knowledge of how God will work in our situation. Instead of trusting that He is the one who is leading and guiding us, the one who is working all things together for our good (Romans 8:28), we question the way God is using our specific situation to bring about His glory.

For example, when Lazarus was critically ill, Mary and Martha sent word to Jesus because they believed that if Jesus came immediately, He would heal their brother. They thought they knew how it should be done and how Jesus worked in these kinds of situations. In their minds, they had it all figured out. But Jesus had something greater in mind. Jesus delayed coming to them. Lazarus died during the delay. Spiritually speaking, we must get rid of our calendars, clocks, smartphones, or ways we think God ought to do things. He might have a better way; in fact, He always has the best way of doing things. We can trust Him, as He knows what to do.

When we choose to do things in our own way, we often complicate the situation. God's delays do not mean that He has forgotten us or our circumstances. Have faith that He has another way that we may have not yet thought of.

Guilt from Sinful Actions

When we have guilt in our lives because of something sinful we've done, it can be hard to believe the Lord offers us complete forgiveness. Our thinking might be telling us, *My sin was too big; God can't forget that.* But that is not the truth.

Many doubt that God *really* forgives them because their sinful acts were too big or lasted for too long. Some have haunting memories of past sins. Even when confessing their sin and asking for forgiveness, they still carry the weight of guilt and shame. They have not yet believed—by faith—that Jesus can and does forgive them (see chapter 18). But John writes, "If we confess our sins, he is faithful and just to forgive us our sins and to purify us from all unrighteousness" (1 John 1:9).

There is nothing we can do to *earn* forgiveness from God. Although we were guilty, Jesus Christ paid for all our sins on the cross. We may still have the memory of our behavior and our consciences may try to trick us into thinking that we have not yet been forgiven, but we must trust in the power of the cross. We might still have to deal with the consequences of what we have done, but the guilt from our sin has been removed.

The enemy of our souls puts doubts into our minds so we will not trust the Lord. Jesus said, "[The devil] was a murderer from the beginning, not holding to the truth, for there is no truth in him. When he lies, he speaks his native language, for he is a liar and the father of lies" (John 8:44).

The devil is always trying to deceive and accuse us. In fact, he endeavors to put thoughts of doubt into our minds because he does not want us to trust God. When we live trusting God, living by faith and believing in His promises, God will give us unique, supernatural favor. Living our lives in fear, doubt, and constant apprehension will often translate into the very thing we fear. Today we can decide to begin trusting God's promises to us. We can decide to have faith in Him and let His promised Holy Spirit help us.

Quieting the Voices of Doubt

When we are in doubt, what do we do? How do we quiet the voices of doubt? We would suggest it comes by focusing on and listening to the voices of faith instead. When doubting, ask yourself some of these questions to help identify where the doubt is coming from:

- Where do these doubts come from?
- When did they start?
- Is there a person in my life who is cynical, caustic, and full of doubt? Has he or she influenced me?
- Has God ever failed me in the past?
- Didn't the Lord promise to meet all my needs in Christ Jesus (Philippians 4:19)?
- Did God give me the Holy Spirit to enable me to believe Him and do whatever He requires of me (John 16:13)?
- Didn't the Lord promise to be with me at all times (Hebrews 16:13)?
- Is anything too big or difficult for God?
- Will this unbelief cost me a lifetime of regret?
- What kinds of situations typically cause me to doubt the Lord? What Scripture passages address these issues?
- Have I ever faced a time where I had more than one choice about what to do? Was it a big choice that determined my future? Did I believe God or allow my reasoning or feelings to determine my choice? What happened because of my obedience or disobedience?

How is your faith today? Is it strong and consistent, or weak and fluctuating between doubt and faith? Is there anything in your life that is causing you to doubt God or His love for you? What can you do to gain strength and confidence in Him?

There are many Christians who are full of doubt and fear. They question whether God's promises will work for them. They might even believe He will work miracles for others but not for them. This type of doubt is paralyzing, but we can choose to not let it keep us from making the choice to believe.

Today, many have lost their peace of mind and have various illnesses, both physical and mental in nature. I (Dr. Cho) have not been able to escape its clutches. During my early adulthood, I passed through a deep valley of suffering when I had tuberculosis and a nervous breakdown. However, with the realization and acceptance of the Bible verses, "Jesus Christ is the same yesterday and today and forever" (Hebrews 13:8) and "I am the LORD, who heals you" (Exodus 15:26), I was filled to overflowing with health and life.[1] You, too, can be filled with hope as you make the decision to trust the Lord, to have faith and believe. Choose now to trust and believe in God and His promises for you.

6

〰

Listening to
the Holy Spirit

"When the Spirit of truth comes, he will guide you into
all the truth, for he will not speak on his own authority,
but whatever he hears he will speak, and he will declare
to you the things that are to come."
—John 16:13 ESV

One day the Holy Spirit impressed upon my heart (Dr. Cho)
that, since the Bible says, "He sent out his word and healed
them" (Psalm 107:20 ESV), "Why don't you give the Word boldly
to the people? Speak the healing. God sends His Word through
your mouth." The Holy Spirit reminded me of God asking Ezekiel
to speak to the dry bones: "Prophesy over these bones, and say to
them, O dry bones, hear the word of the LORD. Thus says the Lord
GOD to these bones: Behold, I will cause breath to enter you, and
you shall live" (Ezekiel 37:4–5 ESV).

"So why don't you speak?" the Holy Spirit asked me.

I thought this must have been an idea that came from the Holy
Spirit. At first I was frightened, but then I was determined to speak.
After I heard those impressions and sensed the encouragement

from the Holy Spirit, I began to boldly speak that a specific person was healed, and that a specific disease was disappearing. And miracle after miracle began to occur. A person who was healed came to me and said, "When you spoke that word, it shook me. Suddenly I felt the healing power flow, and I was healed."

Through my own experience, I have found the wonderful secret that God's creative power is working through our mouths. In the book of Genesis, God spoke and the light appeared, God spoke and the firmament appeared, and God spoke and humankind was created in His image. And later in the New Testament, Jesus spoke and the people were forgiven; He spoke and the sick were healed; Jesus spoke and the devil left; Jesus spoke and the turbulent sea became calm. And as you read about in the Acts of the Apostles, through prayer and the leading of the Holy Spirit, sick people were healed. The apostles and disciples were walking in faith, doing what the Lord had instructed them to do.

By *speaking* in the name of Jesus, people were healed, those who had demons were set free, and mighty signs and wonders took place. When we sense the Holy Spirit encouraging us to act or speak in faith, our words are critical. Peter *said* to Aeneas, "Aeneas, Jesus Christ heals you; rise and make your own bed" (Acts 9:34 ESV). To Paul, Jesus *said*, "Get up and go into the city and you will be told what you must do" (Acts 9:6). And earlier Peter *said*, "I have no silver and gold, but what I do have I give to you. In the name of Jesus Christ of Nazareth, rise up and walk!" (Acts 3:6 ESV).

Amazing miracles happened in the early church. That generation experienced one of the greatest moments of human history. In Jesus' name, the early church spoke healing to the people. But through the passing of time—to the second, third, and fourth generation, until our generation—doubt, misinformation, heresy, false teachers, and doctrines of demons have crept into the church. But Jesus hasn't changed; the Holy Spirit dwells in every believer. When we are full of the Holy Spirit, we have the same power the apostles had. God will use you as you walk by faith and speak words of faith. The same power the early church demonstrated is available to us today. Our sophisticated, cyber-focused, social-networking, post-modern time has not changed or threatened the Creator's power.

Eastern Russia

In 1992, I (Dr. Cho) went to speak in the eastern part of Russia. It was very dangerous and difficult; eastern Russia was in a great state of turbulence. It was far enough away from Moscow that the police protection was loose. I went to a stadium filled with about thirty-five thousand people. The Russian Orthodox Church was there to attack me; some of the Communists were scaring me. On the second day, my hotel was so carefully watched by the KGB that I could not leave my hotel because there was concern I would be assassinated.

I sat in the hotel the whole day, but in the evening I decided to go out. When I picked up my Bible and was ready to leave the hotel, I heard a clear voice—almost audible. It was ringing in my soul: "You are leaving as a living man, but you will return as a dead man tonight. You will be assassinated. You came as a living person to our city, but you will return home in a casket. Don't go to the meeting or you will return home in a casket."

At the time, people were being killed by shootings—every day. So I was preaching behind bulletproof glass that the Russian government had given to me so I wouldn't be killed, which would be a diplomatic problem. However, I knew that people could also shoot me from the back, so while I was preaching, I was conscious of the people behind me. It was a terrible feeling.

When I heard that voice in my hotel room, I had to decide if it was from the Holy Spirit or from the devil. If we don't clearly and quickly discern the voice we hear, then we will be in trouble. I began to think about the predicament that Paul had been in when returning to Jerusalem (see Acts 21). The government and prophets said that Paul would be arrested and put in jail, so he was admonished not to go. But Paul was determined to go to Jerusalem, knowing he would be arrested.

Before my experience in Russia, I always thought that Paul made a great mistake. He should have listened to the voice of those people warning him not to go to Jerusalem. Paul still went because he discerned the voice of the Holy Spirit. Almost instantly I said to myself, *I should not go to the service tonight. I do not want to die. I want to see my wife and children.* I prayed, "God, what shall I do?" Then I heard another voice in my heart; it came with great assurance.

The first voice was loud in my soul, "You are a dead person. Tonight you will be shot. They will carry your dead body to the hotel. Don't go." Then the Spirit said to my heart, "Go to the meeting tonight. You will have great miracles in the service." I said, "You devil, in the name of Jesus Christ, get out of me. To live is Christ and to die is gain. So if tonight I go to heaven, it is okay. I am ready to accept that." Then I left the hotel, trembling from fear.

When I arrived at the stadium a short time later, people were packed in. I was constantly looking behind me as I sat on the platform. Just before I stood up to preach, an ambulance came to the stadium. Usually an ambulance would not be permitted to get close to the stadium. But as the ambulance came closer, I could hear the siren and thought, *Oh, they must have heard that I was going to be shot at and they have come to take me away.* I instantly froze in my chair.

The back door of the ambulance opened, and they carried a man out. He looked like a rich man and one who was in high authority. They put him into a wheelchair and pushed him out among the crowd. The Communist young people began to argue with him, saying, "Why do you come to this kind of meeting? He is preaching false doctrine. There is no living God. You cannot be healed. You are bringing shame on us. We are Communists. We do not believe in God. He is telling a lie. Go back into the ambulance." At that moment, many Christians came and said to the man that Christ is alive. These two groups of people were surrounding this man in the wheelchair and arguing back and forth.

I was inspired and said, "Oh God, if you don't heal this man in the wheelchair, I will be in great trouble. I will be shot at for sure." I then stood up and preached, sensing a powerful anointing from the Holy Spirit. I felt the assurance and confidence that God would honor His Word. The fear I felt was overcome by faith. When I asked for those who wanted to be saved to stand up, to my amazement all thirty-five thousand people stood to their feet.

"Everyone sit down," I said. "You misunderstood me." Then I went on to explain, "All those who want to be saved for the first time, please stand up." Again, thirty-five thousand people stood up.

I asked my interpreter, "Did you say my words correctly?"

"Yes," he said.

I asked him, "Then why do they all stand up?"

He looked at me. "Pastor, these people have never heard the gospel before in their lives. For seventy years we have not heard the gospel of Jesus Christ. They are newcomers. You are from a Western country. You don't know our situation. They all heard the gospel for the first time this evening, and they all want to be saved. Just accept them. Don't question them."

So I led them to Jesus Christ. Then I began to pray for healing. At the time, I had great success in praying for divine healing among the Russian people. Because of the bondage of Communism and the absence of being able to hear the gospel, the people were hungry, humble, and open to the message of Christ. However, that night I was concerned about the Communist gang. Though I preached strongly, and prayed the healing prayer with faith, I was afraid to announce that healings took place: "This man with a deaf ear was healed. This man with arthritis was healed. This person who has stomach trouble was healed."

I could not say that the man in the wheelchair had been healed, however. My interpreter said, "Everyone knows him; he is a great man. He was in an accident and has a broken backbone. He has been in a wheelchair for seven years. They tried every way, but he could not be healed." Before entering seminary, I was preparing to be a medical doctor, so I understood enough about medical possibilities that I thought it was impossible for him to be healed.

The people began to stand up and testify of their healings. This strengthened my faith, so I said, "My brother who is sitting in that wheelchair, you are healed." That was not easy for me to say. That man started to rise but then sat down again. He struggled to rise a second time but sat back down. For a third time he struggled to get up. Very wobbly he started to walk a few steps, and then he began to run and rushed onto the platform, where he hugged me with a typical Russian bear hug. I was being choked. He hugged me and cried, saying, "I am healed. I was sitting in that wheelchair for seven years, and now I am healed."

This man was so excited that he scared me by jumping off the high platform. Then he went to where his wheelchair was and hoisted it into the air and began to walk. The entire stadium was in an uproar.[1] The Communists had completely failed that night, but what a success for the Christians!

Before I left my hotel, the devil scared me. And if I had not heard the Holy Spirit speaking to my heart, I would not have come to the stadium. A positive announcement and declaration of faith is important. If you speak negatively, then you will stop the flow of the Holy Spirit. But when you speak positively, you release the power of the Holy Spirit.

The Holy Spirit Will Encourage Us to Use Words of Faith

When people begin to talk negatively, saying, "I have no power. I have no strength. I have no confidence," then they can do very little. They are telling themselves that they can't and so are full of doubt and unbelief. They are already defeated before they even begin. Instead, always say, "In Jesus Christ I can teach. I can win. My business can succeed. God can give me a creative idea. I can preach and teach. I can do this because I can do all things in Jesus." Even though you think you have no ability in yourself, say, "I can do all things in Jesus. Because of the grace of God, He will help me do this."

Be mindful that your insecurities, fears, doubts, and haunting words from negative people will paralyze your ability to be used of God. Memorize, depend on, meditate on, and believe in the words from Scripture. The miracles the Bible records for your encouragement are possible for you today—if you believe.

When we pray, we need to listen to God and expect that He will answer our prayers according to His will. But we also need to trust that He will give us information and instruction through the Holy Spirit. Many times, He answers us by enabling us to see a vision or a dream so we can live in the vision. Our attitude can be positive; we can hear and see Jesus working. We always need to avoid being cynical or fixating on criticism or doubt. Don't depend on your own personal strengths or abilities; look at Jesus and confess an affirmative confession.

The Holy Spirit will encourage our faith; however, we need to understand how to hear His voice and act in faith. Jesus said that the Holy Spirit would remind us of all that He said (John 14:26). In Christ, we have life abundantly (John 10:10). This is a remarkable truth. Who we are in Christ is powerful and absolutely life changing. It is extremely important to have a positive spirit and never have a defeatist spirit.

We Are Temples of the Spirit and Have the Mind of Christ

The Holy Spirit wants to change our thinking patterns to patterns of faith, hope, and trust in Jesus Christ. As Christ-followers, we have "the mind of Christ" (1 Corinthians 2:16), we are "children of God" (John 1:12), and the Holy Spirit will remind us of what Jesus did, said, and is presently saying to us (John 14–16).

The Holy Spirit will frequently give us hope for our future through a dream or a vision for tomorrow. We have the hope that we will be healed and the hope that we will have the blessings of Abraham so we can be a blessing to others. Those who are lonely can have the hope that they can go to heaven; the Bible says that it will be according to our faith. Some say, "I have nothing, so how can I have a dream?" As you believe, God will give you a dream, a vision, and hope.

When he entered the house, the blind men came to him, and Jesus said to them. "Do you believe that I am able to do this?" They said to him, "Yes, Lord." Then he touched their eyes, saying, "According to your faith be it done to you."

—Matthew 9:28–29 ESV

By faith you can have what you do not have. You can believe by faith you will have employment, your needs will be taken care of, God will answer your prayers, and you can believe for miracles. You can say, "I have faith, and it will be according to my faith that my dream will come to pass." God hears every word we speak. When we pray according to the will of God, then He will remind us of illustrations and truths from His Word and respond to our prayer of faith.

Be specific when you pray. What do you need? Whom are you praying for? Exactly what is it that you want God to do? He has given you a vision, and you can see something that is impossible becoming possible. As you read and study the Scriptures, you will discover truths, principles, and insights about the will of God. At times, the Holy Spirit will give you specific illumination of a particular Scripture, which encourages your faith.

We communicate with others by specific words. By faith, pray this way when bringing your requests to God—use specific words, names, and needs—then your vision and dreams can be your focus as you pray. Remember that you can do *all* things because of God's grace through the cross of Calvary. Through the blood of Jesus Christ, you can become healed and prosper, having tremendous hope for your future.

You Can Depend on the Help of the Holy Spirit

The Holy Spirit will help you walk in faith and encourage you to be positive with the confession of your mouth. As you listen to His voice, He will lead and guide you into all truth. Our thirst for truth, hope, success, contentment, and understanding the purpose of life will be quenched. The Holy Spirit will help you understand life's challenges and turn them into successes.

Like a *spring of water* that overflows, you too will walk in truth, hope, and faith. Jesus told the woman at the well, "Everyone who drinks of this water will be thirsty again, but whoever drinks of the water that I will give him will never be thirsty again. The water that I will give him will become in him a spring of water welling up to eternal life" (John 4:13–14 ESV).

The devil comes to kill, steal, and destroy, but Jesus came to give us abundant life (John 10:10). This is a fulfilled life where you can experience the power of the Holy Spirit and know that God answers your prayers and takes care of your needs. The enemy of your soul desires to bring doubt and unbelief to where you question the truth of the Word or disbelieve in the power of prayer or the dream or vision that the Holy Spirit gives you. The devil certainly does not want you to walk by faith. The power you have through the Holy Spirit is a tremendous threat to the enemy's kingdom. He will try to discourage you and stop you from believing.

We live in a desperate time of global tension, confusion, wars, and moral confusion, where people question or blindly disagree with God's truth. South Korea is under constant threat from the north. As a result, millions of people pray for peace and safety and for their persecuted families and friends who remain in the north.

In our time, many call good evil and evil good. Like in the time of Jeremiah, "They have no shame at all; they do not even know how to *blush*" (Jeremiah 6:15). Doubt and unbelief is common, and thus the world tries to solve the problems with natural ideas and understanding. The confusion of this world will not be solved by humanity's power but by the power of the Holy Spirit.

The Holy Spirit Will Encourage Your Faith

The Holy Spirit will solve these problems as He leads us. When the Holy Spirit is in our workplace, He will prosper it. And if He resides in leaders within a nation, that nation will prosper. Jesus did not leave us as orphans, but He sent the Holy Spirit to us as our Guide, Counselor, and the one who brings hope, wisdom, and knowledge. He works inside of us.

When you fight sin, holiness will be developed in your life. When the Holy Spirit encourages you to trust in Jesus for healing, you will be healed. When the Holy Spirit is with you, then you will have the blessings of Abraham, which means you will be a blessing to others. Jack Hayford wrote:

The Spirit-filled life is the new-dimensional life of worship, witness, and warfare. And the key to its realization is the anointing Jesus places on your life—like heavenly oil poured over the heads of priests, prophets and kings in ancient times. And that anointing is the result of being filled with, overflowed by, and baptized in the Holy Spirit.[2]

You Are a New Person

On the cross, Jesus said, "It is finished" (John 19:30). What did He finish? He paid the price for our sins and we are now justified through the blood of Jesus Christ. We are without accusation, no longer bound to sin but bound to righteousness. We have been forgiven of all our sins—past, present, and future. He is our propitiation. He took our poverty, and through the Holy Spirit He will give us creative thoughts about how to prosper. You are no longer in darkness but have been transferred into the kingdom of His beloved Son.

Through Christ, we are strong, courageous, and have a measure of faith that will grow as we use it. By His stripes we are healed, and we are a blessing to others as we allow the power of the Holy Spirit to be demonstrated in our lives. As Christ-followers, our name is in the Lamb's Book of Life. There is no temptation we are not able to overcome; we are new creations in Jesus Christ.

As you read the Scriptures, your mind is changed and renewed by the power of the Holy Spirit. Draw a beautiful future on the canvas of your heart; as the Holy Spirit leads you, draw a wonderful picture for your tomorrow. Say, "I have faith." For it is faith that will bring wonderful miracles into your life. Jesus said, "If you have faith like a grain of mustard seed, you will say to this mountain, 'Move from here to there,' and it will move, and nothing will be impossible for you" (Matthew 17:20 ESV).

The Holy Spirit Will Help You
Overcome Doubt

There have been many times when I have been frightened about stepping out in faith. In my prayers, I have heard and been encouraged by the Holy Spirit to do or say something I wasn't comfortable with. Throughout the years, the fear that I once had has been greatly reduced as I have repeatedly seen God do what He put into my heart. The Holy Spirit has gently spoken to me on a daily basis, helping me to see in my heart what God can do as I walk by faith.

When Jesus healed me of terminal tuberculosis, I could not imagine how He would use me, but I had a dream that He would use me as I depended on Him. When the Holy Spirit spoke to me about starting a church in an impoverished, destitute, and miserable part of our city, I could not imagine what that church would become, but the Holy Spirit spoke to me about what it could become if I walked by faith. When the church was begun on Yoido Island, the island was largely unpopulated. It seemed to be a bad location. Through the Holy Spirit, however, I saw the population, as well as businesses, government offices, and the tourist industry grow. We would be a light upon a hill to masses of people.

I could not see the church becoming the largest church in the world, nor could I see the influence that it would have on South Korea and the global church. But the Holy Spirit saw it and spoke this hope to me. Together, with the power of the Holy Spirit and by God's grace, untold miracles have taken place. I can't explain the details about how this happens; however, I know that when you have great faith, God hears and responds:

> Though you have not seen him, you love him. Though you do not now see him, you believe in him and rejoice with joy that is inexpressible and filled with glory, obtaining the outcome of your faith, the salvation of your souls. (1 Peter 1:8–9 ESV)

SECTION II

The Faith Hall of Fame

Now faith is confidence in what we hope for
and assurance about what we do not see.
This is what the ancients were commended for.

—Hebrews 11:1–2

7

What Is Faith?

Now faith is being sure of what we hope for,
being convinced of what we do not see.
—Hebrews 11:1 NET

When you have faith in something, that means you believe that it is going to happen. There is a sense of assurance that even though you have not experienced it or have not yet possessed that for which you have faith, it is a reality. Ten-time US national diving champion Laura Wilkinson accomplished her dream to compete in the Olympics. She qualified to participate in the Sydney games in 2000, but about six months before the games, she experienced a tragedy that would cause many to stop believing or give up trying—she broke three bones in her left foot.

The thought that she might not be able to compete was obvious to her and to her team members. For two months, she was unable to train. With the Olympics just four short months away, she found a way to dive again with a special fitted shoe made to help her climb the ladder. She postponed a needed surgery and kept trying—continuing to believe—having a sense it could be done.

She qualified for the Olympic team, and through the eye of faith she proclaimed, "I'm a winner! I can win!" And she won. Laura is a follower of Christ and she memorized and believed Philippians 4:13: "I can do all things through him who gives me strength." She repeated this verse many times a day, envisioning winning and believing that with Christ she could do it. To the amazement of the crowd and the world, Laura won the gold medal for her diving performance off the ten-meter platform.

Laura's 2000 gold medal win was an Olympic moment that demonstrates how people can come from seemingly impossible circumstances to accomplish their dreams. Some ask the question, how did she have such a positive attitude and a sense of hope? It is because she had the faith to believe that Jesus would help her as she trusted in Him.[1]

Difficult to Understand

Faith is difficult to understand because it is unique from our senses of sight, hearing, smell, taste, and feeling. Depending on the translation one uses, faith is mentioned over 450 times in the Bible. Not only that, but it is demonstrated numerous times in the lives of "the faithful" throughout Scripture.

Faith is a quality of life of which every person needs much more understanding—especially us as believers. The only way to live a godly life is by faith. The writer of Hebrews tells us, "Without faith it is impossible to please God, because anyone who comes to him must believe that he exists and that he rewards those who earnestly seek him" (Hebrews 11:6).

If we try to understand God through our senses alone, we become frustrated. If Adam had lived by faith, he probably would not have submitted to the temptation to disobey God when he looked at the fruit with his physical eyes. When Jesus fasted for forty days in the desert and was tested by the devil, He lived by faith and completely trusted in the Word of God. Jesus was victorious over the devil. He did not follow His senses when the enemy tested Him; rather, He trusted His Father.

Our senses are continually bombarded by sensual temptations. Through the Internet, television, movies, and social networking, people are continually hearing the message of believe (and do) what you feel, see, smell, taste, or hear. Scientific thinking and human reasoning are normal ways of determining how to live one's life. Some say the Red Sea couldn't have split, the resurrection could not have happened, and the universe could not have been created by the word of God because these are impossible feats.

People are possessed with the illusion that heaven can be built upon science and the rationale of one's mind. They are drugged with the gospel of human-centeredness. Our human thinking, reasoning, and trying to determine how to live without welcoming our Creator into the equation has not been the answer. In the world today, we live in endless strife, wars, hatred, distrust, ever-increasing crimes, and out-of-control lawless behavior from terrorist groups. Consequently, people do not know the purpose and meaning of their lives. They live aimlessly in terror that they will eventually be destroyed together with this dying world.

Under these circumstances, the only way to live in security, instead of fear, is to live by faith in God. When we come to Christ, we repent of our sins and believe He has forgiven us and cleansed us (1 John 1:9). We change from unrighteous to righteous (Hebrews 10:38) and begin our new life of faith. We are delivered from "the domain of darkness and transferred to the kingdom of his beloved Son" (Colossians 1:13). "Our citizenship is in heaven" (Philippians 3:20); "we walk by faith, not by sight" (2 Corinthians 5:7 ESV).

How Can We Understand and Live by Faith?

Hebrews 11 is often called the "faith hall of fame" chapter. It gives us the only definition of faith in the Bible. Heroes of the faith are listed as examples of people who believed God and trusted Him despite the circumstances in which they found themselves. When reading this chapter, we can see how people like us have made decisions to trust God by faith. We are reminded that it is essential to have faith if we are going to grow in our Christian life.

Faith is what makes the follower of Christ different from non-Christians. As believers, we live and think differently. We frequently make decisions about what to do and how to behave or think that are often different from unbelievers. Henry David Thoreau said, "If a man does not keep pace with his companions, perhaps it is because he hears a different drummer. Let him step to the music which he hears, however measured or far away."[2] The truth is that Christians walk through life listening to another drumbeat.

In Hebrews 11, the focus is on faith. Because faith is misunderstood by many people, it is helpful to understand what faith *isn't*. Faith isn't just following an inclination, or positive thinking, or hoping or wishing for the best, such as, "I hope everything works out for you." It isn't an optimistic feeling. Though these have been identified as faith, the writer of Hebrews isn't describing faith in general but *having faith in God*. Hebrews 11 gives us the ingredients of faith and some demonstrations of faith.

Ingredients of Faith

Faith Creates Hope

The writer of Hebrews says, "Faith is the assurance of things hoped for" (Hebrews 11:1 ESV). To hope is a critical element of living, but discontentment is the frequent feeling of many. When we feel a sense of discontent and are dissatisfied with the way we are, we can be reminded that faith begins with "things hoped for." We might want a better life, a better job, or to live a healthier life. Faith starts with a sense of discontentment. We look at the way things are and long that our marriage, work, or relationships would be stronger, that they would be better.

Your life *can* be better; God can demonstrate His power in your life and through what you do. If you aren't dissatisfied with the way you are, then it will be impossible for you to exercise faith and see your circumstances changed.

One of the greatest enemies of faith is complacency or a sense of being satisfied. It is actually arrogance that says, *I really don't need anything; I don't need to grow or improve.* Many people feel that life—their material possessions, income, people they know, the power that they have, or their prestige—is enough. Or some are fatalists who believe that there is no possibility that things could get better. It could be that many want faith, but they are not ready to have it because there is no sense of dissatisfaction in their lives. If we are dissatisfied in any area of our life, then we look for faith, courage, wisdom, healthy relationships, or doing more for Christ. All of us need to grow and exercise our faith.

Do you want to grow as a disciple of Christ? Would you like to achieve more for good in life? Do you hunger for more wisdom, discernment, favor with God, and creative thinking? Would you like to be a better husband, wife, parent, pastor, employer, or employee? You are looking for something better inside. Dissatisfaction can be our friend as it causes us to hunger and want more from life that has real meaning.

Faith Gives Us Conviction about Unseen Realms

Faith is also "the conviction of things not seen" (Hebrews 11:1 ESV). Not only do we "hope" for something different, but we are also aware that there is a spirit kingdom that we do not see with our physical eyes. Nevertheless, it is real.

In that world, there are activities, spiritual powers, authorities, weights and measurements, things that cannot be touched, and much more. In our physical bodies, we cannot see them, but that does not mean those things are not there. All of this (and more) is as realistic as anything that we can see with our physical eyes. By faith we understand that this spiritual kingdom is real.

Hebrews 11:6 (ESV) says, "Whoever would draw near to God must believe that he exists." Some have said that this is the difficult part Christianity: "Believing in a God you cannot see." But it is more difficult to not believe in God than to believe in Him. When carefully examining our existence, the universe, the meaning of life, and the order of the way things are created, we realize it is truly amazing. Paul writes:

> For what can be known about God is plain to them, because God has shown it to them. For his invisible attributes, namely, his eternal power and divine nature have been clearly perceived, ever since the creation of the world, in the things that have been made. So they are without excuse. (Romans 1:19–20 ESV)

As humans, we can choose to not believe in God or not have faith; doing this takes great effort because we have been created by God in His image. We have been wired by God to know Him; He desires for us to know and live for Him. Ecclesiastes 3:11 says that God "has set eternity in the hearts of men," while Paul wrote that "God our Savior … desires all people to be saved and to come to the knowledge of the truth" (1 Timothy 2:3–4 ESV). Faith gives us a conviction of things that are not seen.

Faith Gives Us Assurance

A third ingredient of faith is "the assurance of things hoped for" (Hebrews 11:1 ESV). We want to be better people—better husbands, wives, workers, and leaders—and so we hope for this. When we have the assurance that we are going to achieve these attributes or obtain what we see by faith, then we begin acting on the revelation that God has put into our hearts.

Faith puts you in touch with reality, with what *really* exists. You begin believing, trusting, and listening to the Holy Spirit, who brings revelation. A whole new and amazing world opens up for us as we put our faith in Christ. We go deeper than human reasoning can take us; we believe God's promises. What an incredible way to live. Faith is not a joke or a crutch to lean on; faith is a reality. It stabilizes your life as you trust God in all that you do.

Examples of Faith

Hebrews 11 gives us many examples of people who walked by faith. Let us look at three people who believed God when the world around them had other opinions. The one's who believed experienced their deepest desire, which was God's approval. The three people we will look at are Abel, Enoch, and Noah.

God Accepted Abel's Faith

> By faith Abel offered to God a more acceptable sacrifice than Cain, through which he was commended as righteous, God commending him by accepting his gifts. And through his faith, though he died, he still speaks. (Hebrews 11:4 ESV)

Cain and Abel were the two oldest sons of Adam and Eve. That world was much different from our own. There was no Internet, no cars to drive, no airplanes to fly in, and no buildings to work in or intense schedules by which to work. Life was less complicated and perhaps easier to understand. But these young men wanted something more—they desired God and all He had for them.

Perhaps it was Adam or Eve who explained to Cain and Abel that they could offer acceptable sacrifices to God. In their attempt to do this, however, Cain tried to shortcut God's will, thinking he could do it his way by offering some fruit from the ground. His thinking and rationalization caused his sacrifice to be rejected. This way of thinking has been around since the beginning of time: *There are many roads to heaven, lots of ways to find truth.* Or, *I'll just live a good life and forget the "God thing" and do my own thing and be happy.* But it is all deception.

On the other hand, Abel believed God and was careful to be obedient to God's formula. The shedding of blood was part of his act of worship. A life must be lost before one can have life in God. He realized that he needed God and would not be blessed unless he gave up his way and depended on God's grace. This young God-seeker understood that he needed God in order to be successful. Abel was the first person to learn this truth, and Scripture tells us he is still speaking to us by his faith. Are we listening?

Enoch Was Taken by God

> By faith Enoch was taken up so that he should not see death, and he was not found, because God had taken him. Now before he was taken he was commended as having pleased God. (Hebrews 11:5 ESV)

Enoch was the seventh man descended from Adam. Genesis tells us that when Enoch was sixty-five years old, he changed his way of living. Something happened that caused him to begin walking with God with much more intimacy. He became a desperate God-seeker and did all he could to be obedient to Him.

Enoch sensed the presence of the God that he could not see with his eyes. All day long he communicated with God, as he knew God was there, walking with him. He walked so close to God that

Scripture tells us that God just took him—he didn't die. He couldn't be found because God translated him to heaven. Enoch is one of two people in the Bible who never experienced physical death. Enoch pleased God because of his faith, and God simply took him to heaven without tasting death.

Noah Built in Faith

> By faith Noah, being warned by God concerning events as yet unseen, in reverent fear constructed an ark for the saving of his household. By this he condemned the world and became an heir of the righteousness that comes by faith. (Hebrews 11:7 ESV)

Noah lived in an out-of-control world. The people had become godless, lawless, and rebellious. God was aware that the people whom He created in His image wanted nothing to do with Him. But Noah stood out in the crowd—he was a God-seeker, a righteous man, one who feared God. He understood that the Creator was in control of history.

God told Noah about future events: the flood would happen, so he was to build a huge ark that would hold his family and a collection of God's creation from the animal kingdom. People mocked him, even laughed at his so-called fanatical belief, but he kept on building because he heard from God. He knew what God had said would come and thus needed to plan accordingly. The ark was built hundreds of miles from the nearest ocean, much too large for only his family.

Noah had the "assurance" that the flood was going to happen, even when it had never happened before and he had no physical evidence that it would happen—only God's promise. As a result, he "became an heir of the righteousness that comes by faith" (Hebrews 11:7 ESV).

We, too, are heirs of righteousness as we believe and trust in Jesus Christ. Faith believes there is another dimension, a dimension that is different from what we touch, taste, see, or feel—it is more than height, width, or depth. The invisible kingdom of God offers to us truths beyond description, answers to life's questions that science or reason alone cannot explain, and a peace that is beyond human understanding.

By faith we believe that God in His goodness, mercy, and grace has created us and has come into human history and given us truths by which to live, facts that doubters do not believe. But we also believe, and we adapt, adjust, and conform our lives and walk in these truths. As people of faith, we are often made fun of, mocked, and informed that we need a crutch on which to lean. They do not understand, however, nor can they ever understand, until they take a step of faith and believe. Even though there might be persecution, mockers, and rejection, the faithful win because we live in reality—in God's kingdom.

What must be asked is this: Where is your faith? Do you need a miracle? Is your life in desperate shape? That feeling of desperation could be the very thing you need. You can decide to trust God and do the right thing; you can begin to walk with God every day and see another dimension of hope and answers to your deepest questions. You can commit yourself to be obedient and walk by faith, much like the heroes of faith in Hebrews 11. Your name and story could be added to that list.

Do You Know Where You Are Going?

In January 2000, leaders in Charlotte, North Carolina, invited their favorite son, Billy Graham, to a luncheon in his honor. Dr. Graham initially hesitated to accept the invitation because he struggled with Parkinson's disease. But the Charlotte leaders said, "We don't expect a major address. Just come and let us honor you." So he agreed.

After wonderful things were said about him, Dr. Graham stepped to the rostrum, looked at the crowd, and said, "I'm reminded today of Albert Einstein, the great physicist who this month has been honored by *Time* magazine as the 'Man of the Century.'

"Einstein was once traveling from Princeton on a train when the conductor came down the aisle, punching the tickets of every passenger. When he came to Einstein, Einstein reached in his vest pocket. He couldn't find his ticket, so he reached in his trouser pockets. It wasn't there, so he looked in his briefcase but couldn't find it. Then he looked in the seat beside him. He still couldn't find it.

"The conductor said, 'Dr. Einstein, I know who you are. We all know who you are. I'm sure you bought a ticket. Don't worry about it.'

"Einstein nodded appreciatively. The conductor continued down the aisle punching tickets. As he was ready to move to the next car, he turned around and saw the great physicist down on his hands and knees looking under his seat for his ticket. The conductor rushed back and said, 'Dr. Einstein, Dr. Einstein, don't worry, I know who you are. No problem. You don't need a ticket. I'm sure you bought one.'

"Einstein looked at him and said, 'Young man, I too know who I am. What I don't know is where I'm going.'"

Having said that, Billy Graham continued, "See the suit I'm wearing? It's a brand-new suit. My children and my grandchildren are telling me I've gotten a little slovenly in my old age. I used to be a bit more fastidious. So I went out and bought a new suit for this luncheon and one more occasion. You know what that occasion is? This is the suit in which I'll be buried. But when you hear I'm dead,

I don't want you to immediately remember the suit I'm wearing. I want you to remember this: I not only know who I am ... I also know where I'm going.'"[3]

Do you know where you are going after your physical life is over? You can know when you give your entire life to Jesus Christ.

Jesus, the founder and protector of faith.

—Hebrews 12:2 ESV

8

Faith:
There Is No Greater Power
in the World

For the prisoner who had lost faith in the future,
his future was doomed. With the loss of belief in the future,
he also lost his spiritual hold; he let himself decline and
become subject to mental and physical decay ... .
The only chance people had of making it in the camps
was their ability to focus on some future goal, it had nothing
to do with who was the healthiest or strongest, but who
had someone waiting back home for them or had some
vocational goal they dreamed of realizing some day.
—Viktor Frankl, *Man's Search for Meaning*

Faith, Hope, and Love Are Intertwined

Faith, hope, and love are qualities that cannot exist without each other. When we have hope, it is intrinsically linked to faith. Likewise, *agape* love cannot be truly exercised without hope and faith. We first need faith to believe, hope to endure with the confidence of God's faithfulness, and God's unique love that is to be part of our

Christian lives. Paul writes, "God's love has been poured into our hearts through the Holy Spirit who has been given to us" (Romans 5:5). These qualities work together as we walk in the Spirit. Without them, we are hopeless and empty.

Every person has enough faith to have eternal life. Within each individual, there is the ability to believe in God and to trust Him. Within you there is incredible potential to succeed and to overcome life's challenges and difficulties (including addictions, failures, and any bondage that the enemy has on your life). You can be greatly used of God.

Every person is created in the image and likeness of God; however, as a believer you are also *a child* of God. He will help you accomplish more than you can imagine—if you believe and trust the founder of your faith, Jesus Christ.

God is love.

—1 John 4:16

While serving in the US Navy, I (Wayde) was stationed on the island of Guam. My job was to work in communications, where I was entrusted with top-secret clearance. That means I could view messages that were highly classified and ensure they got to the right person or military facility. I was loyal to the job that was assigned to me and ensured that I protected the information I saw or heard.

Although I could perform my job with excellence, I was a confused young man. Frequently I thought about the meaning of life and wondered why I existed and what the purpose of life was. I didn't know about Jesus Christ or the promises that are given in the Bible. At twenty-one years old, I was searching for answers to life's questions in all the wrong places. And so I developed unhealthy, destructive habits, such as getting drunk, associating with people who were bad examples, and doing things that were harmful to others and myself.

Another serviceman invited me to attend a church service. Having nothing else to do, I accepted his invitation and visited that small church. The pastor was an Assemblies of God missionary. I watched people as they worshiped, lifting their hands, some with tears in their eyes. They were sincere about what they were doing and seemed at peace in their souls. I sensed the presence of the Holy Spirit for the first time and heard a clear message about Jesus Christ. I desperately needed hope, answers, and peace. And so I returned to the church that evening and the missionary introduced me to Jesus Christ.

That day was the beginning of my faith journey. The missionary gave me a Bible, taught me how to pray, and he, along with many of the people in that little church, sought me out and encouraged me. They explained various Bible passages and Bible truths and offered helpful examples of what I could do to grow in my newfound faith. I craved reading the Bible and memorizing Scripture. Whenever I was with mature Christians, I was full of questions. My hunger to grow in Christ remains to this day.

As believers, all of us started our walk of faith at a particular moment in time. Some people who grew up in a Christian home may feel that they have always been Christians, while others came to Christ later in life after hearing the truth about Jesus Christ clearly presented. The variety of stories of when and how people became followers of Jesus are fascinating.

The Founder and Protector of Faith

I (Dr. Cho) often remind people that "Jesus is the founder and protector of your faith" (Hebrews 12:2 ESV). He created you and, as a believer, will protect your faith in Him. He will also help you grow as you seek Him. As you listen to the Holy Spirit, you will begin thinking and imagining new things that can be accomplished with His strength. He will entrust you with responsibilities that might surprise you. As you trust Him and begin walking by faith, He will use you as an example to others.

Faith and trust go hand in hand. To have faith in God means that we trust Him regardless of the circumstances; to trust means that we have the faith that He will take care of us. The Bible gives us many examples of people who trusted God and had tremendous faith. In fact, Hebrews 11 has been called the "faith hall of fame." More than twenty examples of people who accomplished impossible feats "by faith" are given, encouraging us to have great faith and to believe God for what many think is impossible. God desires that we grow in our faith journey and that we are greatly used by Him.

Hebrews 11 gives details about what the Lord has in store for those who follow Him. As followers of Christ, we can read about the tremendous acts of faith in the Bible and have confidence that if God can use them, then He can use us too. The miracles, mistakes, and life examples given in Scripture are given by the Holy Spirit so we can learn, grow in wisdom, and believe. God has more faith, answers to prayer, and dreams and visions for you.

God's immeasurable grace is beyond human understanding. We must always remind ourselves that His grace is why we have faith in the first place—it enables us to believe for eternity. Paul wrote, "For by the grace given to me I say to everyone among you not to think of himself more highly than he ought to think, but to think with sober judgment, each according to the measure of faith that God has assigned" (Romans 12:3 ESV).

Our "measure of faith" is the criterion by which we appropriately evaluate ourselves, and, most importantly, it is given to us by God. Because we receive a measure of faith by God's allocation, we are prohibited from thinking of ourselves "more highly" than we ought to think.

Along with our measure of faith, the Holy Spirit has given all Christians different charismatic gifts (including the gift of faith). These different gifts, which are outlined in 1 Corinthians 12:1–11, will grow and develop as we utilize faith with the unique gifts that the Holy Spirit has given to us.

I often think about the grace of God in my own life. Many times I have felt that His forgiveness and blessings on my life are undeserved. The wonderful infilling of the Holy Spirit and the boldness to be a witness for Christ is such a powerful gift. God's gifts of healing, prophecy, faith, and discernment are gifts that I depend on each and every day. His gifts are because of His grace alone. None of this is because of our natural abilities, human intellect, or creative thinking. It is all because of God's grace. There is no greater power in the world than the power of faith.

9

Confidence That Builds Faith

True faith is confident obedience to God's Word
in spite of circumstances and consequences.
—Warren W. Wiersbe, *Be Confident (Hebrews)*

aith is a confidence and a witness from within that helps us determine to keep our focus on the unseen God. Paul wrote, "So we fix our eyes not on what is seen, but on what is unseen. For what is seen is temporary, but what is unseen is eternal" (2 Corinthians 4:18).

Faith Is Confidence in God's Promises

Faith is a confidence that God will do for us what He said He would do. Without God, our faith is empty. If we base all our faith on the ability of other people, or on ourselves, we will be disappointed. Everyone (including you) will disappoint you. There are no perfect people in this world. Life can be full of empty dreams and unfulfilled promises; others cannot fulfill your dreams. On the other hand, when a person's faith is connected to God, then it is truly powerful indeed. The Bible declares that what is impossible with man is possible with God (Luke 18:27).

To have faith that something is *certain* is much the same as having hope. Paul writes, "For in this hope we were saved. But hope that is seen is no hope at all. Who hopes for what they already have?" (Romans 8:24). With faith, we are sure of what we hope for, which means we trust that God's promises are true. With hope, we have concluded that something in the future, something God has promised, will actually come to pass because God will make it (or let it) happen.

A common statement from people who don't understand our faith in Christ is, "Your belief in God is a crutch," or "You use faith in God because you are weak as a person." This suggests that faith in something other than one's self is a weakness. Our response to them, or to anyone with other philosophical arguments, is this: "How does your life work without God? Who or what do you trust in, and are you sure they will always be available for you? Do you have the assurance of eternal life?"

When a person leaves the Creator out of the equation, life can be disappointing and fearful. Without God, we totally depend on ourselves or trust other people. How well does that work out for us? Jesus said, "Apart from me you can do nothing" (John 15:5 ESV). Our Christian faith allows us to have confidence in things that we see through our spiritual eyes. By this we know that God is real and fulfills His promises. This is why it is written of Moses, "By faith he left Egypt, not fearing the king's anger; he persevered because he saw him who is invisible" (Hebrews 11:27).

All the people listed in Hebrews 11 had a revelation from God. It came by a word, vision, dream, circumstance, or the Holy Spirit's quiet voice within. Some actually heard God's voice or saw an angel sent by God to speak to them. These revelations encouraged their faith to believe and to have confidence that God would do what He said He would do. Faith is an assurance, a confidence, that God will always do what He has promised to do in and through us.

Faith Is Applauded by God

Faith is commended (or applauded) by God. When we follow the leading of the Lord by faith, God commends us. Our faith pleases Him, and He will give us favor and open doors. Because we trust Him with His Word, and believe Him when He prompts us, we are honored in His presence.

Prayer Mountain is about thirty miles north of Seoul, Korea, which is within seven miles of the North Korean border and in the demilitarized zone. The purpose of Prayer Mountain is to provide a place for people to seek God and to fast and pray for others and themselves. Often those with sicknesses, family problems, or business problems come seeking answers from the Lord. We frequently hear of a miracle, a healing, or some supernatural wisdom resulting from seeking God at Prayer Mountain.

Pastors, deacons, and deaconesses are assigned to Prayer Mountain for specific times to minister in services or to counsel and pray with the people. There are many prayer grottos around the facility where people can pray for longer periods of time. People from Korea, the United States, and numerous other countries come to spend a day, a week, or even longer in prayer. Often as many as a thousand people come at one time to pray.

On one occasion, a businessman came to spend a week in prayer. One of his employees had stolen the payroll that was due to all the employees that week. The employer did not know who was guilty; however, he informed his employees that he would go to Prayer Mountain and take the problem to the Lord in prayer.

During the week, one of his employees came to Prayer Mountain with a sack full of money and announced that he was the guilty one. He said, "Every time I put my hand in the bag, my hand strangely began to tremble and guilt overtook me." The man asked his employer to forgive him and gave him the sack with all the money he had stolen. His employer was an elder in our church and chose to forgive his employee, and then led him to the Lord. The employee is now born again and filled with the Holy Spirit; he, too, became an elder in the church.

God honors faith. He will work in areas that we cannot and will defend and protect us and convict people who have brought us harm. You are His child, and He will give you favor and work on your behalf as you trust Him and do the right thing.

Faith Understands the Mysteries of Creation

Faith understands some of the mysteries of creation. Once again, Hebrews says, "By faith we understand that the universe was formed at God's command, so that what is seen was not made out of what was visible" (11:3).

In human terms, it's difficult to explain miracles, signs, wonders, dreams, visions, and revelations from God. However, God instructed us how He formed the universe, divided the Red Sea, raised the dead, healed the sick, and has given His gifts to people today. Through God's Word, we can understand His will. Without His Word and the Holy Spirit's leading, life is a mystery, and the future is a guessing game. The Bible explains how God created the universe and will also help you know His promises for the future.

Warren Wiersbe writes concerning Hebrews 11:3:

Three words in Hebrews 11:1–3 summarize what true Bible faith is: substance, evidence, and witness. The word translated "substance" means literally "to stand under, to support." Faith is to a Christian what a foundation is to a house: It gives confidence and assurance that he will stand. So you might say, "Faith is the confidence of things hoped for." When a believer has faith, it is God's way of giving him confidence and assurance that what is promised will be experienced.[1]

The word *evidence* simply means "conviction." This is the inward conviction from God that what He has promised He will also perform. The presence of God-given faith in one's heart is conviction enough that He will keep His Word and do what He has promised to do on our behalf.

Faith Obtains a Good Report

Wiersbe continues:

Witness ("obtained a good report") is an important word in Hebrews 11. It occurs in verses 2, 4, and 39. The summary in Hebrews 12:1 calls this list of men and women "so great a cloud of witnesses." They are witnesses to us because God witnessed to them. In each example cited, God gave witness to that person's faith. This witness was his divine approval on their lives and ministries.[2]

There are many mysteries and issues we don't understand. However, the Word tells us that God will reveal His secrets, truths, plans, and warnings to us as we seek Him. Some so-called scholars say that miracles, signs, and wonders are not possible. In their human way of looking at these events, they are determined to find a way to scientifically explain what happened.

A miracle to us is miraculous, but a miracle to God is normal. I'll never forget how the faith of a poor, elderly Chinese woman demonstrated the power of faith. We were desperate for funds to complete the church building. I had much opposition as many felt we were building too large. People hoped that the funds would not come in and that I would be proven wrong in my belief that God told me to build this large of a church.

We were two days from when the mortgage payment was due. The congregation had always been generous, but there was almost no response. I stressed the urgency of the need and waited. The people remained unmoved. Like most leaders, I, too, was afraid, but I believed that somehow we would experience our miracle. I prayed as I made a third appeal for funds.

Quietness was in the framed building as many people sat on mats and blankets on the floor. Slowly, from the back of the congregation, an old Chinese woman walked toward the front. In her hands was a battered metal rice bowl and her chopsticks. Quietly and reverently, she handed them to me. "I want to give these," she said.

I knew she was a refugee without any family. Her home was a hovel made of scraps of wood and tin. She begged or worked at any available odd job to get a little rice for her food. "But mother," I said, "I cannot take your rice bowl and chopsticks. They are all you have."

"Yes," the woman replied. "But I can eat from a cardboard box with my hands."

I did not want to take her rice bowl; she looked at me, and I saw her sincere desire to give it as an offering. She said, "Cannot a poor person give? Please sell the bowl and put whatever it brings toward the payment." Tears were in my eyes as I received her gift of the bowl and chopsticks. I knew she gave all she had.

From all over the church, businesspeople and professionals came to the front. They wept as they filled the rice bowl with checks and cash that would more than make the mortgage payment. One of the men bought the rice bowl for more than ten thousand dollars. He said, "I want to be reminded of what it means to give your all to Jesus."

Our faith can powerfully affect those around us. We walk, lead, and live by faith. It can encourage others to keep trying, trusting, and believing. It is an example to many people we will never meet until we get to heaven. This poor woman changed our church.

Hebrews 11 is full of examples of people who made the decision to trust and believe. Even when there was no evidence, they saw something others did not see. They were certain that God was with them, and no matter what they trusted God.

Choose to Believe

We live in a complicated, confused, and dangerous time. In South Korea, we live under constant tension concerning the threats that come from north of our border. Without faith, we live in fear. Our church prays constantly for our brothers and sisters in North Korea. We believe that the prayers that continually come from Prayer Mountain are having tremendous impact on the north. We are building a hospital in North Korea, as we believe that God wants us to help the people.

As those mentioned in Hebrews 11 believed by faith, you, too, can choose to believe:

- If people are against you, believe God.
- If the evidence looks bad, believe God.
- If you have no idea how you will make it, believe God.
- If you are discouraged, believe God.

You have nothing to lose. Have faith and see the impossible become possible. Know that God can do anything. Stand firm and hold steady as you trust and believe. And remember, "I can do all things through him who strengthens me" (Philippians 4:13 ESV).

10

⚜️

The Demonstration
of Faith

Whoever walks with the wise becomes wise,
but the companion of fools will suffer harm.
—Proverbs 13:20 ESV

Wisdom is contagious, but so is foolishness. Therefore, it's important to be cautious about the people with whom we have significant relationships. We can help (or minister to) the doubtful, the cynical, the foolish, and the skeptics, but to bring them into our lives as close friends can cause injury to our faith. Faith can be caught when people and their stories of faith inspire us; one of the best ways to grow in faith is to walk with the faithful.

Hebrews 11:4–40 gives us a summary of men and women who had great faith. We learn that:

- God spoke to them through His Word.
- They were impacted in different ways in their spirits.
- They made the decision to be obedient to what God had spoken to them.
- God bore witness to them.
- Their faith worked.

Unbelievers frequently say that faith is not practical, but the Bible instructs us that faith is very practical (Hebrews 11:3). In fact, faith gives us the ability *to understand* what God does and the ability *to see* what others do not see (vv. 7, 13, 27). As a result, faith gives us the ability *to do* what others do not do. J. Oswald Sanders said, "Faith enables the believing soul to treat the future as present and the invisible as seen."[1]

The Key to Righteousness

Faith is the key to righteousness, for our righteousness only comes through faith in Jesus Christ. Hebrews 11:4 tells us, "By faith Abel offered God a better sacrifice than Cain did. By faith he was commended as a righteous man, when God spoke well of his offerings. And by faith he still speaks, even though he is dead." It is important to see that Abel was a righteous man because of his faith. He understood the true way to worship God and thus lost his life for his faith (see Jesus' words in Matthew 23:35). His brother did not have faith and was not a child of God (1 John 3:10–12). Cain had religion, but he did not have righteousness. Abel was the first martyr of the faith, and he communicates to and inspires us still to this day.

All of us have the same "unrighteousness" problem; we have sin that needs forgiveness. Having faith in Jesus and repenting of our sins is the solution to this problem. On the cross, Jesus paid the price for our sins. Thus, we are forgiven, cleansed, justified, have no accusations, are declared righteous, are the elect, and are saints who belong to Christ Jesus. With this born-again experience, we become children of God. Without Christ, we are not capable of living a righteous life. Proverbs reminds us of this when it declares, "The path of the righteous is like the morning sun, shining ever brighter till the full light of day" (Proverbs 4:18).

Very much like Abel, your acts and prayers of faith continue to be powerful even after you have physically died. If you die before you see the promises of God fulfilled, or before you see answers to prayers that you have been faithful to pray, then your words, activities, prayers, example, and courage will continue to have an impact on others long after you are gone.

Faith Is Our Path to Heaven

Faith is our path to heaven. The Bible teaches us that walking by faith is the way to heaven and eternal life.

People want to know the way to heaven. Having faith in Jesus Christ is the only way to have eternal life. Paul wrote to Timothy, "For there is one God, and there is one mediator between God and men, the man Christ Jesus" (1 Timothy 2:5). There is only one way to heaven, and that is through Jesus Christ.

You see, faith pleases God, and He rewards those who seek Him: "And without faith it is impossible to please God, because anyone who comes to him must believe that he exists and that he rewards those who earnestly seek him" (Hebrews 11:6). Some might say that it's unfair to demand that we have faith before we can please God. Remember that God created you in His image, and that your decision to believe in Jesus Christ enables you to be a child of God (John 1:12). He is full of grace and truth (v. 17).

We are children of grace when we accept Christ as our personal Savior. Other religions require impossible tasks, are cruel, disrespectful, harmful to women, or give the false notion that *in another life* the adherent will return and either become better or worse (reincarnation). Some religions have so many demands that many give up because they cannot fulfill all the requirements to get in.

For decades, our ministry in Korea has grown in amazing ways as God has moved through signs and wonders throughout the years. The major religions of Korea are animism, Buddhism, Confucianism, and shamanism. I (Dr. Cho) knew our people needed not only the wonderful, miraculous power of God, but they needed to diligently study the Bible too. To help them, I wrote many Bible study manuals. Through the study of specific Scriptures, the people learned how to follow Jesus Christ and let go of their beliefs about other religions.

Our lives will take a thrilling turn when we seek Him and remain faithful to Him. Our salvation comes to us when, by faith, we believe in Jesus Christ. For the Bible declares, "If you confess with your mouth, 'Jesus is Lord,' and believe in your heart that God raised him from the dead, you will be saved" (Romans 10:9). All of us can do this—we simply trust God and believe that our faith in Jesus Christ is the only way to please Him.

Many think they are not good enough to become a Christ-follower. You do not need to work, perform, accomplish much, or even become a good person to please God. He already deeply loves you—before you were even born. Your faith in Jesus Christ is all that is needed. With that, you are born again and are a new creation in Christ. God will help you work on the other things as you mature in Him. He will help you overcome bondage, have victory over the enemy, acquire wisdom, and give you strength to live a righteous life. He will open wonderful doors for you.

The writer of Hebrews says that He "rewards those who earnestly seek him" (Hebrews 11:6). To *reward* means to give money or another kind of payment to (someone or something) for something good that has been done.[2] When you trust God to keep His promises, He will reward you for your faith. He will give you visions, dreams, and new goals for your life. The Holy Spirit within you will counsel, encourage, and comfort you. God will reward you by fulfilling His promises and helping you do all that He asks you to do. As you trust Him, He will perform wonderful miracles and go before you and create situations that will help you.

Most people believe there is a God, but many don't know who He is. They don't personally know Him. Deists believe that God exists, but they don't believe He cares about them. They might think that God created the world; however, they assume He is not personally involved in their lives. They might even say that God created everything, but He left it to run by itself. As a result, many deists have become calloused, narcissistic, and hardened because of the evil in the world (see Matthew 10:29). They have difficulty with challenging questions having to do with suffering or injustice.

Until the return of Jesus Christ, we are living in a confused, fallen world that is deeply troubled by sin. Unrighteous people who make wrong and sinful decisions, and the devil and his demons, have an unimaginable impact on the world. Our solution is that we believe God deeply loves us, desires to forgive us, has mercy on us, and blesses our lives. He so personally loves us that He sent His only Son to die for us (John 3:16). God is looking for people of faith who are committed to Him and desire to be obedient: "For the eyes of the LORD range throughout the earth to strengthen those whose hearts are fully committed to him" (2 Chronicles 16:9).

Faith Is Revealed through Obedience

Faith is revealing itself through our actions of obedience: "By faith Noah, being warned by God concerning events as yet unseen, in reverent fear constructed an ark for the saving of his household. By this he condemned the world and became an heir of the righteousness that comes by faith" (Hebrews 11:7 ESV).

Noah might not have understood why he was told to build an ark, but he obeyed nevertheless. Abraham might not have understood the reasons why he was instructed to leave his country and go to another place, but he obeyed anyhow. He walked toward Canaan, a land he didn't know. Although Moses might not have understood the reasons why he was asked to do certain things, he chose to obey God by keeping the Passover and by obeying numerous other requests from God.

The faith that saves you is the faith that will help you obey God daily. God will specifically speak to you about how you can obey Him through your decisions about how to live, how to determine what is right or wrong, and how to treat others. He will speak to you about actions that He desires you to take in your life.

Many ask, "How do I know that this thought or vision is from God?" God will never contradict His written Word, so when you sense that the Holy Spirit is speaking to you, find support for that impression in the Scripture. Also, remember that God often confirms His will to us through other godly people and circumstances.

When determining the will of God, we can always look to the Scripture, receive counsel from wise, godly people, and look for situations that the Lord has brought into our lives. When we feel the Lord's direction, we simply step out by faith and obey. As we are obedient, the Holy Spirit will give us details about how to move forward and what decisions to make.

So also faith by itself,
if it does not have works, is dead.
—James 2:17 ESV

Faith is boldly walking in the direction that God leads, even when we don't know where the road is going: "By faith Abraham, when called to go to a place he would later receive as his inheritance, obeyed and went, even though he did not know where he was going" (Hebrews 11:8). The truth is that there is no safer or more secure place than the will of God. This doesn't mean that the road will be easy, that we will completely understand what we are doing at any given time, or that we will know the details of the future. There will be difficulties and storms that greatly challenge us. If we try to live life by trusting in our own abilities or solely relying on others, then we will always be disappointed. It is dangerous to try to live without having God's favor. When God leads us, He always goes before us. He will always give us the ability to do what He asks us to do.

Never will I leave you;
never will I forsake you.
—Hebrews 13:5

Life in Eternity

Faith believes that where you live life on this earth is less important than where you will live for eternity: "By faith [Abraham] made his home in the promised land like a stranger in a foreign country; he lived in tents, as did Isaac and Jacob, who were heirs with him of the same promise. For he was looking forward to the city with foundations, whose architect and builder is God" (Hebrews 11:9–10).

Abraham was willing to live in a tent while he waited to inherit all that God had promised him. At times, we might go through years of waiting, believing, and trusting before we see the results. We continue to be certain that what we have hoped for will come in God's perfect timing. Our eternal home is waiting for us.

There are times when we do not see clearly what God has promised, but we understand that as we trust Him we will one day see clearly. This is why Paul could write, "So we fix our eyes not on what is seen, but on what is unseen. For what is seen is temporary, but what is unseen is eternal" (2 Corinthians 4:18). Faith is keeping our focus on God's promises:

Against hope Abraham believed in hope with the result that he became *the father of many nations* according to the pronouncement, "*so will your descendants be*." Without being weak in faith, he considered his own body as dead (because he was about one hundred years old) and the deadness of Sarah's womb. He did not waver in unbelief about the promise of God but was strengthened in faith, giving glory to God. He was fully convinced that what God promised he was also able to do. (Romans 4:18–21 NET; see also Hebrews 11:10–11)

There are times when we look back and can see how God was working in our lives, and how His promises and leading were fulfilled. We can see how He worked things for our good through miracles, healings, open doors, favor, godly advisors, protection, supernatural interventions, and so much more. He has truly been faithful.

We still live in the world and contend with our humanity. We make mistakes, make bad decisions, and need to deal with our sinful nature. All of us have said words we regret, have participated in activities that we wish we hadn't, and have times we would like to do over. With these experiences, we trust the forgiveness that comes through the price that Jesus paid for us on the cross. He will always forgive us when we ask (1 John 1:9). But we also need to learn how to forgive ourselves, which seems more difficult at times. Those who don't forgive themselves continue to live in the guilt of the past, which paralyzes our faith. Our only hope is to trust in the forgiveness and cleansing that Jesus Christ brings. Paul wrote, "One thing I do: Forgetting what is behind and straining toward what is ahead, I press on toward the goal to win the prize for which God has called me heavenward in Christ Jesus" (Philippians 3:13–14).

Faith understands that we are aliens on earth because we belong to another country called heaven: "All these people were still living by faith when they died. ... They admitted that they were aliens and strangers on earth" (Hebrews 11:13). We have "eternal life"; our existence goes on after our physical body dies. Every true Christian is a citizen of another country (Philippians 3:20).

The Bible often reminds us that we are strangers on this earth because our true citizenship is in heaven (see 1 Peter 1:1; James 1:11; 1 Corinthians 7:29–31; 1 John 2:15–17; Romans 12:1–2). When our physical life is ending, our faith has confidence and will help us have peace. We know that to be away from our body is to be "present with the Lord" (2 Corinthians 5:8 KJV). Jesus Christ took the power of death from the devil. He destroyed the panic, fear, and apprehension so many have about dying. When our physical life is over, it is not truly over because we are immediately with Jesus.

Faith Anticipates

Faith is looking to and anticipating God's supernatural interventions, for nothing is impossible with God. God encouraged Abraham to try to count the stars in the sky because this number would be like the number of descendants he would be given over generations. When God said this, Abraham was elderly and had no children. In fact, it was physically "impossible" for Abraham and Sarah to have children, but God supernaturally intervened.

We need to believe God's promises. He will speak to your heart and give you dreams and visions of what He will help you accomplish as you obey His Word. Your life is eternal and His promises will continue from this physical life into eternity. Many believers have children or loved ones who do not yet know the Lord. When we pray for their salvation, we know that God answers our prayers even if we don't live to see the fulfillment.

I lift up my eyes to the hills—
where does my help come from?
My help comes from the LORD,
the Maker of heaven and earth.
—Psalm 121:1-2

Faith understands that when God promises something, it will happen—in His time and in His way. "All these people were still living by faith when they died. They did not receive the things promised; they only saw them and welcomed them from a distance. And they admitted that they were aliens and strangers on earth" (Hebrews 11:13).

Our time schedule is twenty-four hours a day, 365 days a year, and a lifetime of "our time." However, God's timing is not our timing. Be assured that His promises will come to pass. Hearing His voice, direction, and promises will help us know His will. When we study His Word, hear the voice of the Holy Spirit, and know the will of the Lord, then we only need to believe and leave the timing up to Him. Many times there is a gap between the promise and the fulfillment.

Faith is having the necessary connection that we need for discernment, wisdom, prophecy and, at times, the ability to know about future events. The writer of Hebrews writes:

> By faith Isaac blessed Jacob and Esau in regard to their future.
>
> By faith Jacob when he was dying, blessed each of Joseph's sons, and worshiped as he leaned on top of his staff.
>
> By faith Joseph, when his end was near, spoke about the exodus of the Israelites from Egypt and gave instructions about his bones. (Hebrews 11:20–22)

There are many times in life when we need to proclaim (speak) what the Holy Spirit reveals to us. Our natural mind might doubt and tell us not to believe or speak about the promises of God, but we can have a sense of assurance that His will or direction will come to pass.

We have a boldness by faith that overcomes fear: "By faith Moses' parents hid him for three months after he was born, because they saw he was no ordinary child, and they were not afraid of the king's edict" (Hebrews 11:23). The act of fearless faith by the parents of Moses is remarkable. Amram and Jochebed were slaves who were commanded to kill their baby (Exodus 6:20). When Pharaoh demanded that all the male babies be thrown into the Nile River, they chose to have faith in what God would do if they trusted Him. Because of their faith, Moses was used in powerful ways.

Fear is a common emotion for all of us. Fear often comes when we are in danger, or if we are uncertain or insecure about our future. At times, this fear comes because of sickness, or of what people would think of us, or of our faith looking like foolishness, or because of an inability to do something that God asked us to do. We can fear for our own lives or for people we deeply care about. When we have faith, we trust God to take care of us and to intervene in the lives of those we care about and pray for.

> *There is no fear in love.*
> —1 John 4:18

Our faith will give us strength and boldness. We can trust God when we are persecuted and start again when we fail. When we're mocked for our faith, we cling to His promises and sense God's approval. God will take care of us. We have the assurance that we will always have enough food, clothing, and peace, even in the face of death, as we trust Him.

> *I will never leave you, never will I forsake you.*
> *So we say with confidence. "The Lord is my helper,*
> *I will not be afraid. What can mortals do to me?"*
> —Hebrews 13:5-6

Faith's Values

Faith is being persistent as we trust in Him: "By faith [Moses] left Egypt, not fearing the king's anger; he persevered because he saw him who is invisible" (Hebrews 11:27). Moses had faith that God had asked him to do something unique. God performed many signs and wonders and gave Moses the Holy Spirit's anointing and authority. On numerous occasions, Moses needed to be persistent in the promise God had given him. Pharaoh didn't respond as Moses thought he would, and the community that he was called to lead was frequently rebellious and difficult.

When the promises of God seem to be delayed, if our prayers do not seem to be answered, when people get in the way of the will of God, we can still trust God. Even when something happens that changes our plans, we can still trust God. Through our eyes of faith, we see Him who is invisible and know that God will accomplish His will in and through us.

Faith is being loyal to other believers: "By faith, Moses, when he had grown up, refused to be known as the son of Pharaoh's daughter. He chose to be mistreated along with the people of God rather than to enjoy the pleasures of sin for a short time" (vv. 24–25). Moses could have chosen to enjoy the pleasures of success in Pharaoh's kingdom, but instead he decided to be loyal to his God and the community of God.

We are in a unique kingdom; we are no longer part of the kingdom of darkness. Loyalties, integrity, faithfulness, and commitment to do what we said we would do are characteristics of how we treat others. We are part of the body of Christ and care for one another and demonstrate truth to a confused world. We are loyal to our brothers and sisters in Christ.

Our values and behavior are different when we become a Christian. When we have faith in God, He continuously speaks to us about our personal lives, values, behaviors, and decisions. The choices we make in life are different because we know Christ. Faith helps us persevere and fight (Moses persevered because he saw Him who is invisible). All of us go through testing and the trials of life. With patience, we persevere because we believe His promises.

"By faith [Moses] kept the Passover and the sprinkling of blood, so that the destroyer of the firstborn would not touch the firstborn of Israel" (v. 28). Faith trusts God's way of accomplishing His will. For example, Moses and the children of Israel needed to trust God's instruction for protection. Exodus 12:13 tells us of the Passover, when the Lord passed over the houses of the Israelites and all the firstborn Egyptians were destroyed. We, too, need to trust God's unique ways of accomplishing His will. Too often we compare ourselves with others, which causes us to be confused and sets us up for failure. God created you and has given you wonderful and unique gifts. You can trust His direction in your life.

Moses and the children of Israel saw the Red Sea split in two as they walked through on dry ground: "By faith the people passed through the Red Sea on dry land; but when the Egyptians tried to do so, they were drowned" (Hebrews 11:29). The people were full of fear as the Egyptian soldiers were approaching them. But God wanted them to see that He had His way of delivering them. Our anticipated presumptions will often fail us, but our faith will bring us success.

Faith Believes

Faith believes. Even when people question our faith, we still obey God: "By faith the walls of Jericho fell, after the army had marched around them for seven days" (Hebrews 11:30). We can assume that the people questioned the need for walking around Jericho for seven days before they would have victory. But Joshua obeyed God. Thus, God performed the miracle of victory and deliverance.

At times, people will question our acts of faith, our dependence on God, and our trust that He will take care of us. When unbelieving people question us, we trust God. Noah kept building the ark when people laughed at him (Genesis 6); Peter threw out the net even though they had fished all night and caught nothing (Luke 5:5); people rolled away the gravestone while Lazarus was still dead (John 11:38–44); and scoffers mock our faith that Jesus will return, calling us foolish (2 Peter 3:3–4).

Faith can change anyone who trusts in God: "By faith the prostitute Rahab, because she welcomed the spies, was not killed with those who were disobedient" (Hebrews 11:31). Rahab was a prostitute, but God changed her life. Three times the New Testament speaks of Rahab and how she became a follower of the Lord (see Matthew 1:5; Hebrews 11:31; James 2:25). She left her life of prostitution and became a godly woman who is listed in the genealogy of Jesus Christ. Her faith in God sanctified her, and she became a pure woman. Jesus' genealogy in Matthew 1 tells us she married Salmon, one of the two spies she saved. Rahab became part of the ancestry of Jesus. God radically changed her life.

Contagious Faith

These examples of faith are contagious. I (Dr. Cho) have often thought, "What God has done for others, He can do for me." When I purchased an old discarded tent from the US Army and started a church, I also purchased a cowbell and hung it on a tree and used the sound of the bell to call people to early morning prayer.

The tent was torn and obviously had been used much, but I knew that God was part of the vision to start this church in a tent. We placed rice mats on the ground for people to sit on. I used an apple crate that we covered with a white cloth for my pulpit. I emphasized and reminded the people of the importance of prayer, because I knew that it was prayer that healed me of tuberculosis. And I instructed the people that we were going to pray every day for the numerous needs of everyone who had lived through the war. I encouraged them to come during the day and stay and pray as long as they could and leave when they had to find food for their families.

Every night, I went to the tent church to pray behind the covered apple crate. At five in the morning I rang the bell and waited for a few people to come. I preached to them and prayed with them, and together we believed God. After about three years, there was a breakthrough as God miraculously manifested His power through signs, wonders, and miracles.

During one of the Sunday services, I announced to the few people that I would pray for the sick that evening. I encouraged them to bring the sick so God would heal them. After I announced this, I became terrified, wondering, *What will happen if no one is healed?*

That night many new people came. After I preached, again I told the people that God was going to heal. I was personally struggling with faith and doubt; the fear was still there. Three people came to the front of the little church. The first person was deaf. After praying with him, he began to shout that he could hear! The second and third persons were also deaf, and God healed them too.

Faith and faithfulness are contagious. We believe and trust God even though we doubt. God will do what He promised. He will do what He said He would do. Even though we were in a small war-torn tent, the church grew. God was moving through signs and wonders, and opening the Word of God to the people. They left the services with hope. Like a magnet, the Holy Spirit drew the sick, the wounded, the demon possessed, the hopeless, the poor, and the people in bondage to our precious Lord.

You, too, can begin believing the promises of God. His miraculous power is available to you as you pray. God has given us many examples throughout His Word to encourage our faith. If He did for these men and women of faith, then He can surely do it for us as well!

11

❧

Heroes of the Faith: Things Are Not as They Seem

For we were so utterly burdened beyond our strength that
we despaired of life itself. 9 Indeed, we felt that we had
received the sentence of death. But that was to make us rely
not on ourselves but on God who raises the dead.
—2 Corinthians 1:8-9 ESV

In my sermons, I (Dr. Cho) have tried to highlight the necessity of prayer and faith. I understand that through faith believers would discover the ability to find the answers to their serious questions in life. When we talk about acts of faith, the results of our faith, and how God responds to our faith, many will be encouraged to step out in faith.

During one of our rainy seasons, the downpour lasted for two to three days. The Kang River rose to a dangerous level and flooded areas of Seoul. Two young boys were having fun and decided to walk in the heavy rain through the fast currents of water as it drained. The rain was so intense that the boys could hardly see in front of them. Suddenly, one of the boys disappeared! His friend turned around to look for him and saw an uncovered manhole. He looked inside and saw his friend "sitting" on something as the water rushed by him—but it did not sweep him away. Quickly, he ran to his family's home cell leader who lived nearby.

"Come quickly, come quickly!" he shouted to the leader. She grabbed her raincoat and umbrella and ran with him to the open manhole. Looking inside, she saw the child in a sitting position, but … sitting on what?

She prayed, "Oh God, please stop the rain!" The rain soon subsided.

Some men who were on the street heard her praying and came over to the manhole and saw the child sitting there. Somehow they lifted him out of the hole and were amazed that he was still alive as the level of water was high as it rushed through the manhole.

"Just before I fell in," the boy reported, "a tall man with a white robe said to me, 'Grab the rope and hold on,' and I did. But when I opened my hand, there was no rope." There had not been a rope, but an angel of the Lord somehow provided a rope for the child to hold onto. A home cell leader reported this testimony of God's miraculous intervention, encouraging the people to trust God for all their difficult situations. Today, the child is a businessman living in Australia.

Incredible Victories of Faith:
Hebrews 11:31–40

Hebrews 11:33–35 tells us of incredible victories that came to people who had faith. Six men and the prophets are listed with brief comments about them: "And what shall I say? I do not have time to tell about Gideon, Barak, Samson, Jephthah, David, Samuel and the prophets" (v. 32). Through faith, some achieved great success for the nation of Israel. They believed God, and "through faith conquered kingdoms, administered justice, and gained what was promised" (v. 33).

> Gideon (Judges 6:12–16; 7:7)
> Barak (Judges 4:5–7, 14)
> Samson (Judges 13:5)
> Jephthah (Judges 11)
> David (2 Samuel 7:8–16)
> Samuel (1 and 2 Samuel)

Some of them were delivered from death: "Who shut the mouths of lions, quenched the fury of the flames and escaped the edge of the sword?" (vv. 33–34). When weak, they found a way to connect to God's power and anointing: "Whose weakness was turned to strength; and who became powerful in battle and routed foreign armies. Women received back their dead, raised to life again" (vv. 34–35). The writer of Hebrews continues:

> There were others who were tortured, refusing to be released so that they might gain an even better resurrection. Some faced jeers and flogging, and even chains and imprisonment. They were put to death by stoning; they were sawed in two; they were killed by the sword. They went about in sheepskins and goatskins, destitute, persecuted and mistreated—the world was not worthy of them. They wandered in deserts and mountains, living in caves and in holes in the ground.
>
> These were all commended for their faith, yet none of them received what had been promised. (vv. 35–39)

The martyrdom of the "others" stands in stark contrast to the tremendous miracles, deliverances, and demonstrations of power that are previously listed. As you mature in Christ, you will begin to understand that your life in Jesus is eternal. We are told that there are more martyrs today for the faith than at any time in church history. Since the first century of the church, there have been seasons when Christians have been mocked, tortured, and killed for their faith.

Pentecostal author, composer, and statesman Jack Hayford predicted:

> American Christians shouldn't expect to escape coming persecution in an increasingly wicked world. American churchgoers can't ignore the reality that hundreds of Christ followers in the Middle East are dying for their faith. Christians in the U.S., especially the young, will face persecution, to the point of martyrdom.
>
> My prayer is for an awakening in our land right now. But the evil that is sweeping over our world will increase. The Holy Spirit's empowerment will be necessary to stand unto death.
>
> My prayer is that none of us be seen as merely promoting conformity to a ritual "baptism in the Holy Spirit" to fulfill a creed or a denominational tradition. The world is coming unglued, darkness is deepening and the glow of the Light of the World fills our hearts. But penetrating the darkness—now as then—will require the flames of Pentecost—and not only for a day.[1]

Although Pastor Hayford spoke this specific word to Christian leaders, it is also a word for the twenty-first-century church.

In Korea, we certainly understand the possibility of persecution as the threat of the region is ever upon us. In our church, we have many who have escaped the clutches of persecution in the north. They tell chilling stories about what they've endured, the lives that have been lost, and the danger that other believers live with. But with their persecution, their faith has grown to a deep level that few Christians understand.

It seems that the enemy of our souls is attacking the church like never before. The return of the Lord could come quickly as the signs of His return are evident. The enemy knows that his time is short, so he will do everything he can to disrupt the church and our faith. Be assured that no matter what comes to your life, "the one who is in you is greater than the one who is in the world" (1 John 4:4).

At Prayer Mountain, people pray twenty-four hours every day. Even though there is a constant threat from North Korea, we love and pray for the people and believe that God will one day bring peace to that land. We want to help our brothers and sisters, our friends and relatives, and look for ways to do this. The threat only encourages us to pray more and to believe God.

God's power is available to do all He has asked us to do through faith. The book of Judges often reminds us that the Spirit of the Lord came on the judges with power (3:10; 6:34; 11:29; 14:6, 19; 15:14). As it happened back then, it can happen for us today. Through the Holy Spirit, we have power and boldness (Acts 1:8), power to live a holy life (Romans 8:1–17; Galatians 5:16, 22–25), and power for spiritual gifts of prophecy, healings, and miracles (1 Corinthians 12:4–11). Your faith and trust in God will give you a new focus and power to believe that He will miraculously work in your life.

Faith can operate in the life of any person who will dare to listen to God's Word and do God's will.

—Warren Wiersbe, *Be Confident (Hebrews)*

Faith unites the Old Testament believers with the New Testament believers. The writer of Hebrews goes on to say that "these were all commended for their faith, yet none of them received what had been promised, since God had planned something better for us so that only together with us would they be made perfect" (Hebrews 11:39–40).

Hebrews 11 lists many who pleased God by faith—Abel, Enoch, Noah, Abraham, Isaac, Jacob, Joseph, Moses, the Israelites crossing the Red Sea, Rahab, Gideon, Barak, Samson, Jephthah, David, Samuel, and the prophets. These believers under the old covenant will be made perfect with believers under the new covenant. We are united with these people of faith; we can have the same depth of faith they had. All of them were spoken to through visions, dreams, angelic visitations, God's audible voice, or a deep sense that the Holy Spirit was leading them. We can study how they heard from God, and how they made the decision to believe God, and then reap all the same incredible results.

As they had faith then,
so we have faith today.

These precious Old Testament saints give us courage to believe, trust, and hold steady in a confused and dangerous world. We can look to these men and women of God who trusted and believed, and we can do the same and expect the same results. They stood on their faith in times of difficulty and received "the better blessing" (Hebrews 11:40).

This kind of faith is possible for each and every believer. Our faith will grow as we listen to God's Word (Romans 10:17). Faith is available for every situation, problem, or task that seems impossible. It is not just for the elite believers; it is for all who believe.

Let the saints of old encourage your faith today. They trusted God by faith, so we are told of a sea that is split, time that stood still, an ax-head that floated, people who were resurrected from the dead, the healing of illnesses (blindness, lameness, and leprosy), an angel opening closed doors and loosening chains for an apostle in prison ... and hundreds of other examples from Scripture. They all point to a wonderful God who will act on your behalf—if you have faith.

When I (Dr. Cho) was a child, sometimes I would get into a fistfight with other boys, and every now and then I would come home crying. My mother would give me a good spanking, but it was always followed by a healing touch from a mother who loved me. How good it feels when we are discouraged and a dear friend comes and takes hold of our hands or pats us on our back. Jesus comes to us, and when He touches us, we can't help but receive healing.

Jesus wants to use your arms, your mouth, and your hands. When you lay your hands on the sick in the name of Jesus, the power of the Holy Spirit flows through you to that sick body and healing comes. The Bible says that when you lay your hands on the sick, they shall recover (Mark 16:18).

Within a year after I was married, I discovered my wife had a terrible case of tuberculosis. She was already pregnant; the doctor wanted me to permit an abortion, but it was against my convictions. Every day I laid my hands on her body, and I felt the power of the living Christ flow through her as I claimed the victory. After a few months, she was completely healed.

Shortly after our first son was born, he began to have terrible coughing spells, and the doctor could not cure them. Every evening he would cough until he choked; the doctor was quite worried. Then, in the name of Jesus Christ, I laid my hands on him, and I felt healing power cover him. Over and over when I laid my hands on him, I felt Christ's life flow into him; soon, to the amazement of the doctors, he was completely healed.

God has His hand on your life. As a follower of Christ, the Holy Spirit dwells in you, and when you reach out in the name of Jesus in love and faith to touch Him, His power will flow in and through you. People will be healed, lives will be changed, deliverance will come, and wisdom will be given. Let the healing power flow like a river through you.

Encouraging Our Faith

Hebrews 11 is uniquely given to us to encourage our faith. As you read the examples of people who are used of God, begin thinking, *God can use me too. I too am going to walk by faith. I am going to believe and not doubt, and trust God despite the circumstances or what people tell me. God has given these examples of tremendous faith to me.*

SECTION III

Walking by Faith

The Christian faith isn't just a set of beliefs or a list of rules—it's a personal relationship with the living God! He is now your heavenly Father, and you are now His child. And just as children want to be with their earthly father, experiencing his love and learning from his wisdom, so your heavenly Father wants you to be with Him, experiencing His love and learning from His wisdom.[1]

—Billy Graham

12

⌒⌒⌒

Faithfulness:
The Foundation of Faith[1]

For millennia, the North Star has shined brilliantly, giving direction to land travelers, sailors, and pilots. When south seems to look like north, and east seems to look like west, many look for the North Star because they know they can trust it. People also have always enjoyed watching shooting stars, which seem to come out of nowhere. As quickly as they catch our attention, they fade and burn out. Though they are beautiful, they are not a dependable compass like the North Star.

The fruit of faithfulness (faith in action) is trustworthiness and steadfastness of character in the life of a believer. The Greek word for this fruit, *pistis*, is translated, among other things, as "faith, belief, and trusted." Those who are faithful are dependable, and we can place our trust in them.

God is our best example of faithfulness; He will never break His promises to us. Paul reminded his friend Timothy that even "if we are faithless, [God] will remain faithful" (2 Timothy 2:13), for it is His nature. You can absolutely trust Him and His Word. Not doing what He said He would do is out of the realm of possibility for Him.

God wants us to be faithful like Him, and as with the producing of all fruit, this is possible only as we stay connected to Jesus, the Vine.

We are to be faithful in our relationships with our spouses, children, parents, employers, employees, and friends, as well as people in general. Most of all, we are to be faithful in our obedience to the Lord. One day when we meet Him face-to-face, we will not be judged on our success, our educational achievements, or even on all that we may have given. We will be judged only by how faithful we were to do what God asked us to do. We want to hear the beautiful words, "Well done, good and faithful servant!" (Matthew 25:23).

Being Friends with God

Abraham was called God's friend (Isaiah 41:8). What an amazing thought! We all know—or should know—that God loves us. He desires a relationship with us, and, in fact, believers are called His children (John 1:12–13). But being God's friend is a different kind of relationship, unique in its level of trust and respect. Friendship involves openness in communication, vulnerability, transparency, and a sharing of ideas, dreams, and goals. It is special and should be cherished.

Why was Abraham called God's friend? "Abraham believed God" (James 2:23), and God could count on him to be faithful in all that He asked him to do. The fascinating story of Abraham gives us example after example of a man who simply trusted God at His word and was passionate about being obedient even when He didn't understand how the outcome would come about.

Jesus called His disciples friends. He said, "I no longer call you servants, because a servant does not know his master's business. Instead, I have called you friends, for everything that I learned from my Father I have made known to you" (John 15:15). Friends share information and communicate on a deeper level than mere acquaintances. They trust that if something shared needs to be confidential, then it will be. Friendship involves dependence, relationship, respect, and confidentiality.

Jesus said to His disciples, "You are my friends if you do as I command" (John 15:14). Why did He add a requirement? This has to do with trust. Jesus knows what is best for us. He knows what will work in our lives and what will injure us. Doing His will is doing what will help us in the long and short run. When people don't obey God's principles, they not only show that they want to "do their own thing," but they also show that they do not trust God. They wonder if God is right or if He will come through for them. With friendship comes trust, the assurance that the friend will keep his or her word.

You may say, "How can I be called a friend of Jesus? I will wrestle with temptation and sin and am by no means perfect. Why would He want to be friends with me?" Those of us who love Christ desire to do better and be more like Him. We all deal daily with temptation and strive to be more Christlike in our actions, thinking, and feelings. He understands our motives. He sees potential in us that many of us would not believe, and He sees promise in the worst of sinners. And we should too.

Phillip Yancy writes in his book *The Jesus I Never Knew*:

> When Jesus came to earth, demons recognized him, the sick flocked to him, and sinners doused his feet and head with perfume. Meanwhile he offended pious Jews with their strict preconceptions of what God should be like. Their rejection makes me wonder, Could religious types be doing just the reverse now? Could we be perpetuating an image of Jesus that fits our pious expectations but does not match the person portrayed so vividly in the Gospels?
>
> Jesus was a friend of sinners. He commended a groveling tax collector over a God-fearing Pharisee. The first

person to whom he openly revealed himself as Messiah was a Samaritan woman who had a history of five failed marriages and was currently living with yet another man. With his dying breath he pardoned a thief who would have zero opportunities for spiritual growth. ... I view with amazement Jesus' uncompromising blend of graciousness toward sinners and hostility toward sin, because in much of church history I see virtually the opposite. We give lip service to "hate the sin while loving the sinner," but how well do we practice this principle?[2]

We Christians are all sinners who have been saved by grace. Some of us have stories that we aren't anxious to tell, but before we came to Christ, Jesus saw something in us. He decided to take a risk on us and attempt friendship even though we were not living for Him and could reject His love. He chooses to remain our friend even though we are not perfect. He understands our struggles and continually prays for us and stays loyal to us.

The idea of being a friend of God is puzzling to many believers. But if you have given your life to Christ, that is what you are—His friend. Are you trying to develop this friendship? Do you communicate your deepest concerns, worries, and struggles to Him? Do you want to be with Him? Do you want to be more like Him? Do you trust Him?

Like Abraham, we are friends of God. Our faith is to be like Abraham's. He was obedient to God and trusted Him. We, too, must be obedient to God and trust Him in all that we do.

Faithfulness Is a Sign of Maturity

One of the main qualities I (Wayde) look for when choosing a person to run a program or lead a department is whether candidates are faithful to do what they say they will do. This may be demonstrated in their completing assigned tasks in the time period we have discussed, or, if there is an unforeseen obstacle, speaking to me about it so it can be resolved in a timely manner.

I notice if they are disciplined with their time, if they keep their word, if they complete the job, and, in the process, if they treat people well. Does it seem that being responsible is critical to them, or do they just do the job because they are interested in the financial remuneration? One major sign of immaturity is a person's refusal to accept responsibility.

Our children may want money and privileges of being an adult, but if they cannot handle money correctly or get up in time for school, college, or their job, they have not learned responsibility, and it is not wise to give them privileges. A lot of people want to be supervisors, managers, and leaders, but any employer who puts people in charge who don't understand responsibility will injure the organization.

God's kingdom is organized in such a way that if we are faithful in the small things, we will be given more responsibility (Matthew 25:21, 23). Spending time reading and studying the Bible, being consistent in our prayer lives, and obeying God's will are all part of maturity in Christ. God has given all of us certain responsibilities. When we disobey or refuse to accept what God has asked us to do, we are unfaithful. But doing all that God asked us to do is a sign of spiritual maturity.

You may say, "I have a long way to go in this area of faithfulness." Perhaps you feel frustrated by your failure to follow through on some commitments you have made. One of the greatest truths you can understand is that you can improve. You will become more faithful to God and godly commitments as you are transformed into Christ's likeness.

Paul wrote to the Galatian believers, "I am again in the pains of childbirth until Christ is formed in you" (Galatians 4:19). The word *formed* (Greek *morpho*) means the inward and real formation of the essential nature of a person. Paul would agonize until Christ was formed in these believers. His concern was that they would demonstrate the character, or fruit, of Christ. This Greek term was used to describe the formation and development of an embryo in a mother's womb.

Paul wrote in Romans 12:2, "Do not conform any longer to the pattern of this world, but be transformed" (Greek *metamorpho*). This word is the root for the English word *metamorphosis*. A caterpillar is formed and developed (transformed) into a beautiful butterfly. Likewise, as we grow in the grace of God, we are transformed and we become more faithful, loving, and gentle. This fruit is more evident in our lives after years of walking with Christ than in the beginning when we first became Christians.

If you are concerned that you are not faithful enough or do not have enough joy or that you do not love people with the depth that you feel the Lord wants you to, then understand that when you walk in God's Spirit you are being transformed, and as you grow you will develop. But you must hunger to grow in His fruit and determine to permit God to form Christ within you.

Dr. Lewis Sperry Chafer, the founder of Dallas Theological Seminary, was a creative, visionary, and unique individual. On one occasion, he was asked to speak at a banquet. The audience had sat through three hours of preliminaries, such as announcements, music, presentations, and acknowledgements. Sensitive to the time, Dr. Chafer stepped up to the podium and began.

My subject is the Reasonableness of Fully Surrendering Our Lives to God. Reason number one: He is all-wise and knows better than anyone else what is best for my life. Reason number two: He is almighty and has the power to accomplish that which is best for me. Reason number three: He loves me more than anyone else in the world loves me.

Conclusion: Therefore, the most logical thing the Christian can do is to surrender his life completely to God. What more can I say? What more need I say?[3]

That was his message, and what a powerful message it was! He could have talked for hours—and put everyone to sleep—but the truth rests in the simple fact that "the most logical thing the Christian can do is to surrender his life completely to God." When we do so, fruit, such as faithfulness, will naturally become apparent in our lives.

The Story of Faithfulness

In the parable of the talents (Matthew 25:14–30), Jesus gave us two examples of people who were faithful and one who was not. The two who were faithful took what their master gave them and invested it wisely. The third man either was afraid of his master or was lazy and didn't take advantage of the opportunity that was given him. Possibly he was both.

We can learn at least four truths from this parable: God gives everyone different gifts, more responsibility is good, people who are lazy with God's talents are punished, and only people who invest get a return.

God Gives Everyone Different Gifts

Jesus said, "To one he gave five talents of money, to another two talents, and to another one talent, each according to his ability" (Matthew 25:15). Some people have many talents and are capable of multiple responsibilities. In the parable, the master determined the amount of talents each servant was capable of handling well. The master was only concerned about how each man used the talents he was given.

Some have the idea that God will give greater rewards to those who have incredible gifts and abilities. However, this is a wrong assumption. God rewards us according to how we use our gifts. He is watching our stewardship as we develop and invest the gifts He has given us. God will never say, "I wish you had that gift and used it for my kingdom." He doesn't compare us to anyone else. God will reward us according to how we used what we have been given. We do not have the same talents, abilities, or gifts as others; however, we possess the same ability to be faithful with what we have.

More Responsibility Is Good

The master said to his servants who invested his money, "Well done, good and faithful servant! You have been faithful with a few things; I will put you in charge of many things" (Matthew 25:21, 23). The two servants who invested their talents well received more responsibility, yet all responsibility was removed from the one who did nothing with his talent.

In God's kingdom, responsibility is given to those who can handle it. Will your attitude be humble? Will you work hard with what you have and remain loyal to the process? If something needs to be done and no one else will do it, will you be willing to move forward without hesitation? If so, God will help you in your effort to do well. You will be able to look back with gratefulness that you stepped out by faith.

In his book *When God Whispers Your Name*, Max Lucado tells the story of a man named John Egglen who had never preached a sermon in his life:

Wasn't that he didn't want to, just never needed to. But then one morning he did. The snow left his town of Colchester, England, buried in white. When he awoke on that January Sunday in 1850, he thought of staying home. Who would go to church in such weather?

But he reconsidered. He was, after all, a deacon. And if the deacons didn't go, who would? So he put on his boots, hat, and coat and walked the six miles to the Methodist church.

He wasn't the only member who considered staying home. In fact, he was one of a few who came. Only thirteen people were present. Twelve members and one visitor. Even the minister was snowed in. Someone suggested they go home. Egglen would hear none of that. They'd come this far; they would have a service. Besides, they had a visitor. A thirteen-year-old boy.

But who would preach? Egglen was the only deacon. It fell on him.

And so he did. His sermon lasted only ten minutes. It drifted and wandered and made no point in an effort to make several. But at the end, an uncharacteristic courage settled upon the man. He lifted his eyes and looked straight at the boy and challenged: "Young man, look to Jesus. Look! Look! Look!"

Did the challenge make a difference? Let the boy, now a man, answer: "I did look, and then and there the cloud on my heart lifted, the darkness rolled away, and at that moment I saw the sun."

The boy's name? Charles Haddon Spurgeon. England's prince of preachers.[4]

Some people do not want more responsibility. In fact, they look forward to getting rid of it. In God's kingdom, however, we are always asked to put forth a 100 percent effort to use the gifts God has given us.

People Who Are Lazy with God's Talents Are Punished

The servant who had one talent did nothing with it except bury it, forget about it, and go on with his life. His master called him lazy and wicked: "Take the talent from him and give it to the one who has ten talents. ... And throw that worthless servant outside, into the darkness, where there will be weeping and gnashing of teeth"

(Matthew 25:28, 30). He could have at least deposited it with the bankers and received some interest, but he didn't even have the discipline to do that.

We all know people who work hard and have much to show for their efforts. Not long ago I (Wayde) stayed at the beautiful home of a Romanian immigrant who had moved to the United States with his family just a few years earlier. When they arrived in the United States, they had few material possessions and were poor, but they were determined. Over the years, they have been faithful to God, have worked hard, have invested well, and are givers. They now own more than a hundred rental apartments and use their talent in business to bless God's kingdom.

This ability came to them one dollar at a time and one apartment at a time. They were anything but lazy with what God had given them. They did not say, "I have so little, how can I make it in America?" They said, "Look at all the possibilities in this land of opportunity. With God's help, we can invest what we have and receive great interest." They worked hard, invested wisely, and have given the glory to God.

Only People Who Invest Get a Return

Jesus finishes up the parable by saying, "For everyone who has will be given more, and he will have abundance" (Matthew 25:29).

Farmers know they must plant their seed by faith, water it, and take care of it. If they do not plant it, then they will have only weeds in their fields. "Use it or lose it!" This truth has a parallel to God's kingdom. When by faith we use the talent God has given us, care for it, and work at it, we will get better and be given more. That will never be taken from us. People who practice get better. If, however, we decide not to be faithful with our God-given talents, they will be taken from us.

In 1972, NASA launched an exploratory space probe called

Pioneer 10. The probe was designed to reach Jupiter, take pictures, and transmit the information back to earth. This bold effort required that the probe not only travel the distance (no probe had ever gone past Mars) but that it also would need to pass through Jupiter's magnetic field, radiation belts, and atmosphere. One of the major concerns was that *Pioneer 10* would be destroyed going through the asteroid belt before it could reach its destination.

As we know, *Pioneer 10* fulfilled its assignment. In fact, when it flew by Jupiter in November of 1973, the planet's tremendous gravity pitched the probe with greater speed into the solar system. At one billion miles from the sun, the tiny probe passed Saturn then flew past Uranus at some two billion miles. By 1997, twenty-five years after NASA said good-bye to *Pioneer 10*, it was more than six billion miles from the sun.

This probe that was designed to be useful for approximately three years continued to signal back to earth from incredible distances far beyond its original assignment. Jaroff writes, "Perhaps most remarkable, those signals emanate from an 8-watt transmitter, which radiates about as much power as a bedroom night light, and take more than nine hours to reach Earth."[5] Today, we look back on this remarkable feat—this idea that became bigger than life. After more than thirty years of communicating, the last signal from *Pioneer 10* was received on January 23, 2003. The scientists who created this remarkable probe did not imagine its potential.

Similar to *Pioneer 10*, we have tremendous potential to be more than we may think is possible. As we remain faithful to what God has given us and continually strive to be obedient to His will, He will stretch us and develop us in many ways. As Charles Swindoll has said:

> Don't expect wisdom to come into your life like great chunks of rock on a conveyor belt. It isn't like that. It's not splashy and bold ... nor is it dispensed like a prescription across a counter. Wisdom comes privately from God as

a by-product of right decisions, godly reactions, and the application of spiritual principles to daily circumstances. Wisdom comes … not from trying to do great things for God … but more from being faithful to the small, obscure tasks few people ever see.[6]

What can you do? What has God blessed you with? How are you investing it for God's glory? Are you lazy or are you growing in maturity? Don't waste the talent God has given you.

Keeping Our Commitments

I (Wayde) am often asked to give recommendations for persons who want jobs, particularly ministry positions. At times, I am hesitant to recommend persons because they have had a history of not fulfilling commitments. They have quit too soon, left their previous position in the wrong way, or left things undone so that it was difficult for the person who followed them. Instead, I must caution the person or church that is interested in the individual. On the other hand, when people have been faithful to do their best and have fulfilled their commitments, I can give outstanding recommendations.

Dependability, punctuality, and being responsible are all part of the package of faithfulness. Jesus said, "Whoever can be trusted with very little can also be trusted with much, and whoever is dishonest with very little will also be dishonest with much" (Luke 16:10). When your employer, supervisor, or friend counts on you to do something, do you come through?

We face challenges in the work we do that require our faithfulness. For instance, sometimes our work is boring or tedious. I have talked to people who have kinds of jobs where this issue is a real concern. Perhaps they flip hamburgers for McDonald's. My advice to them is, "Be the best hamburger flipper you can be. Study the art of flipping hamburgers. Ask great burger people how they do it so well, and become an expert in the field." We can find a challenge in everything we do, but most of the time it depends on our attitude.

Another challenge is the amount of work we are asked to do. At times, it seems overwhelming. Add to the amount of work the interruptions of e-mail, text messages, phone calls, and coworkers. I have met people who simply do not answer their e-mails or text messages or phone calls. My personal policy is to try to return every message or call the day it is received. If I can't, then I ask my assistant to let the person know when I will be able to respond to his or her communication. If I don't have time to give a complete answer to someone's question, I briefly respond and let the person know that I will respond to their communication (in more detail) soon. When the people have taken the time to ask a question, voice a concern, or give a kind word, they deserve a response.

We also need to be trustworthy with the finances of the organization for which we work. Some with expense accounts spend much more than they would if using their personal finances. We need to be good stewards and try to live as we would with our own budgets. Being sensitive to your employer is part of being faithful. Jesus asked, "If you have not been trustworthy with someone else's property, who will give you property of your own?" (Luke 16:12).

Your employer has hired you for a particular amount of time each week. Do you show up on time? Do you take too many breaks and long lunches? Do you leave early? What about those for whom you don't directly work but assume you will be careful with what they own? How do you treat rental cars, hotel room accessories, or something you have borrowed? Are you trustworthy?

Faithfulness is practical in the way it is lived out. It is a lifestyle that people depend on and that God is aware of when He sees it in our lives. Paul instructed the Colossian believers, "Whatever you do, work at it with all your heart, as working for the Lord, not for men, since you know that you will receive an inheritance from the Lord as a reward. It is the Lord Christ you are serving" (Colossians 3:23–24).

The late Ray Steadman relates an incident that shows the eternal results of faithfulness:

> An old missionary couple had been working in Africa for years, and they were returning to New York City to retire. They had no pension; their health was broken; they were booked on the same ship as President Teddy Roosevelt, who was returning from one of his big-game hunting expeditions.
>
> No one paid attention to them. They watched the fanfare that accompanied the President's entourage, with passengers trying to catch a glimpse of the great man.
>
> As the ship moved across the ocean, the old missionary said to his wife, "Something is wrong. Why should we have given our lives in faithful service for God in Africa all these many years and have no one care a thing about us? Here this man comes back from a hunting trip and everybody makes much over him, but nobody gives two hoots about us."
>
> "Dear, you shouldn't feel that way," his wife said.
>
> "I can't help it; it doesn't seem right."
>
> When the ship docked in New York, a band was waiting to greet the President. The mayor and other dignitaries were there. The papers were full of the President's arrival, but no one noticed the missionary couple. They slipped off the ship and found a cheap flat on the East Side, hoping the next day to see what they could do to make a living in the city.
>
> That night the man's spirit broke. He said to his wife, "I can't take this; God is not treating us fairly."

His wife replied, "Why don't you go in the bedroom and tell that to the Lord?"

A short time later he came out from the bedroom, but now his face was completely different. His wife asked, "Dear, what happened?"

"The Lord settled it with me," he said. "I told him how bitter I was that the President should receive this tremendous homecoming, when no one met us as we returned home. And when I finished, it seemed as though the Lord put his hand on my shoulder and simply said, 'But you're not home yet!'"[7]

The reward for faithfulness is knowing that you have been obedient and understanding that one day God will say, "Welcome home, my faithful servant!"

13

Hope

Therefore, preparing your minds for action, and being
sober-minded, *set your hope fully on the grace that will be
brought to you* at the revelation of Jesus Christ.
—1 Peter 1:13 ESV

As a young man beginning a lifelong ministry, I (Dr. Cho) could
see wonderful possibilities in people's lives. I didn't understand
then that this was faith—faith in what God could do with a life that
seemed hopeless. The people were poor, sick, broken, and without
hope. As I looked into the eyes of the people in this small church,
I saw only suffering, hunger, sickness, and helplessness. But in my
thoughts, which I discovered were inspired by the Holy Spirit, I saw
the people as healthy, successful, and beautiful.

I was growing in faith and believed that all things were possible in Christ. My heart was excited with an unusual, powerful
affection for these people that became a driving force of love and
compassion. I was filled with the desire to fill their hearts with hope
through Jesus Christ. As I taught this small group of wounded and
bound people, I began to see lives changed—people were healed
and delivered. They became full of hope.

People continually ask me to speak, preach, and talk about hope. If there is a critical need today, it is giving hope to a desperate, discouraged, and disillusioned generation. As believers in Jesus Christ, we should try our best to raise hope in the people with whom we come into contact. This isn't false hope—the hope I am talking about is absolutely real.

When I was dying of tuberculosis, I had no hope at all. When I was within weeks of death, I began reading the Bible and discovered that Jesus was a healer (Matthew 8–9). I did not discover the power of hope in Bible college; it was before my Bible education that I discovered hope—while I was dying. As I read the Bible, I realized that Scripture continually tells us about a healing God who is full of hope for the future and personally involved in people's lives. He cares about even the small things and has a purpose for our lives. This gave me hope.

The doctor said to me during this time, "You have a short time to live—try to eat and try to be happy because you are going to die." But when I read the Bible, hope arose within me that Jesus would heal me, and my mind thought of what I read in the Scripture, not the hopeless words of the doctor (or many in my family).

Jesus performed so many healings and miracles while He was physically present upon the earth. As a young Christian, I didn't understand theology, the Bible, or the wonderful work of the Holy Spirit. I was naive and didn't know what Jesus as my Savior meant (I thought He was a doctor). But when He physically healed me, I understood that I could believe in Him as my Savior and all this entailed.

During this time of reading the Bible and being healed, I also felt that the Holy Spirit spoke to me and reminded me of what I had read in 1 Peter: "By his wounds you have been healed" (1 Peter 2:24). I realized that Jesus took our sins in His body on the cross so we might die to sin and live a righteous life.

No one can deny the healing power of Jesus Christ and that He gives hope to all who are without hope. I said, "Jesus, you are real, you are the Son of God—I believe." I still had some symptoms of the terminal tuberculosis, but when I coughed up blood I laughed at it because I had hope. My thinking was changing from fear to faith as I understood that these symptoms were not of God. It is the enemy who brings the fear of death, accuses us of sins of which God has forgiven, and tries to persuade us to not have faith. I said, "I am healed because of Jesus." When I had bad days and symptoms of the illness, I said to myself, "I am not going to fear." Hope took me through the dark times.

The truth is that all us need hope. If we continually watch or listen to the news that is full of discouraging information, fearful threats of terrorism, war, and economic collapse, then our hope will be greatly injured. If we are listening to people who are full of fear, doubt, criticism, slander, and gossip, then we will be impacted by their conversations. Even if we are ill, or in need of a miracle, we need to look for hope. With God all things are possible. All of us need people of faith in our lives, people who can pray and believe. Jerome Groopman wrote concerning hope:

> Hope is one of our central emotions, but we are often at loss when asked to define it. Many of us confuse hope with optimism, a prevailing attitude that "[t]hings turn out for the best." But hope differs from optimism. Hope does not arise from being told to "think positively," or from hearing an overly rosy forecast. Hope, unlike optimism, is rooted in unalloyed reality. ... Hope is the elevating feeling we experience when we see—in the mind's eye—a path to a better future. Hope acknowledges the significant obstacles and deep pitfalls along that path. True hope has no room for delusion.[1]

Think of when the Lord spoke to Moses from the burning bush. God was calling Moses to be the man who would lead the children of Israel out of slavery in Egypt. Moses didn't realize how much pressure he would undergo as he followed God's assignment. He had incredible odds to face and the pressure was tremendous. Pharaoh could mobilize hundreds of thousands of trained military men who would come after the children of Israel with weapons of war. Israel was not armed or prepared for battle. The people were frightened and backed into a corner. They knew the Egyptians would punish them beyond imagination. Moses said to the people of Israel, "The LORD will fight for you, and you have only to be silent" (Exodus 14:14 ESV). Moses had faith that what he hoped for would happen.

In my entire ministry, I (Dr. Cho) have not tried to explain healing or miracles. God is the healer and the one who performs miracles—I simply decided to believe His Word and obey. When reading the Scripture, I simply ask the Holy Spirit to stamp on my heart the promise of healing and I make the decision to believe without question. When things seem hopeless, I pray and ask the Holy Spirit to fill me with a dream or vision to see the hopeless situation disappear and fill that thought with hope.

The Scripture tells us that even with Lazarus (the dead friend of Jesus), our Lord refused the hopeless situation (in people's eyes), and "cried out with a loud voice, 'Lazarus, come out!'" (John 11:43). The faith Jesus displayed was His dependence on the hope that He knew would happen—Lazarus would awaken from death.

Desperate Faith Means We Have
No Other Place to Go

Not long ago I was asked to speak in Europe on evangelism. Many theologians came to the event, supposedly interested in receiving evangelistic blessings and truths. However, these scholars were not focused on winning the lost; rather, they wanted to argue with my theology. I did not argue but remained quiet. I didn't want to be defensive or endeavor to get into an apologetic debate.

The well-known theologian Jürgen Moltmann was there and commented, "What is the job of the theologian? Theologians help the pastors logically believe." He went on to say, "In my life, I can't find a better theologian than Dr. Cho, and I recognize him as a theologian." With these encouraging words, I could discuss the miraculous—healing, dreams, and visions that the Holy Spirit gives—with the people there.

Moltmann has been called the greatest theologian of our own day. He encourages ministers to speak more on hope and is deeply impressed to help people understand that the hope of the Christian faith is hope in the resurrection of the crucified Jesus. For him, "hope and faith depend on each other to remain true and substantial; and only with both may one find not only a consolation in suffering, but also the protest of the divine promise against suffering."[2]

Dr. Moltmann came to Korea recently and said, "This world is suffering because of a lack of hope. Without hope, they act as if they have no hope; young people need hope—with that they can succeed. I am 100 percent behind Dr. Cho, who continually gives hope."

Totally without hope one cannot live. To live without hope is to cease to live. Hell is hopelessness. It is no accident that above the entrance to Dante's hell is the inscription: "Leave behind all hope, you who enter here."

—Jürgen Moltmann, *The Experiment Hope*

Faith, Hope, and Love

Paul writes, "So now faith, hope, and love abide, these three; but the greatest of these is love" (1 Corinthians 13:13 ESV). The relationship of these three Christian qualities—faith, hope, and love—is frequently mentioned in Paul's writings (see Romans 5:1–5; Galatians 5:5–6; Ephesians 4:2–5; Colossians 1:4–5; 1 Thessalonians 1:3, and, of course, faith and hope also appear together at the beginning of the great faith chapter, Hebrews 11. This kind of faith is steady, optimistic, and hopeful—a confidence in God. Our hope anticipates and looks forward to experiencing answers to prayer and God's miraculous intervention.

"Now faith is the assurance of things hoped for, the conviction of things not seen" (Hebrews 11:1 ESV). When we have this kind of faith, we live through this life full of hope. The writer of Hebrews does not give a definition of faith, but he asserts that faith gives reality—"the assurance of things hoped for"—and firm evidence—"the conviction of things not seen."

Today, we believe in miracles, healings, and all the gifts of the Spirit. When we are in heaven, spiritual gifts, faith, hope, and patience will cease to exist. They will no longer have purpose or meaning there. When we depart from this body and are changed, we will have an imperishable body, we will see Jesus face-to-face, and our faith and hope will be realized. Love will always be the most important virtue. Demonstrating love, therefore—being focused on being loving—and doing the loving thing is always the most important. Throughout eternity we will live in God's love.

Fighting Hope

Many followers of Jesus think God could never use them or help them. There are pastors and leaders who are doubtful that they can be used of God to bring hope, strength, and healing to the people they serve. The enemy has continually attacked them with doubt and discouragement.

Memories of failure, tragic experiences, heartache, or rejection have persuaded a large part of the body of Christ (the church) to not believe in themselves. They look at their future and are full of doubt and expectations of more of the same painful memories. Some become cynical, caustic, and angry with those who believe in God's supernatural interventions. Hope is seldom in their hearts because of the memories of the past. Sometimes these people are not open to healing of their painful memories and thus think that it is too late. They are more comfortable with the accusations of the past than the assurances of the future.

If this is you, or if you have days like this, then we want to ask you some questions and give you helpful principles on how you can become hopeful and overcome the negative image that you have of yourself or your situation.

What Are You Thinking About?

Many allow themselves to continually think negative thoughts. They feel that their physical condition is hopeless, their business is finished, or no one loves them. Our imaginations can get out of control and obsessed with doubt and hopeless thinking. God frequently works through our imagination, however. As long as one permits this onslaught of doubt and hopeless thinking, then he or she is blocking God's ability to help. Our ability to imagine is strong—many times, it can be stronger than willpower.

The psalmist declared, "From their callous hearts comes iniquity; their evil imaginations have no limits" (Psalm 73:7). And Isaiah said, "All day long I have held out my hands to an obstinate people, who walk in ways not good, pursuing their own imaginations" (Isaiah 65:2).

The Scripture teaches us about the importance of our imagination. From the first human beings (Adam and Eve), we see how imagination can be used for good or for evil. Eve was tempted by satan to eat fruit from the tree that God instructed Adam and Eve to not eat from. She allowed the words of Satan to become part of her thinking process, which filled her imagination. Eve continued to think and look at the fruit, and, as a result, her mind rationalized and began to think of the fruit as good. With that thought, she was attracted to the forbidden fruit and had a strong desire to eat of it. And her imagination became reality when she took the fruit and ate it. Despite her willpower, she rationalized and gave in. She then persuaded Adam that the fruit was good to eat and he ate what God had forbidden. They disobeyed God. Through this one act, both Adam and Eve fell. Because of their sin, they developed the self-image of fallen people and their hope for the future became fearful. They would never be the same again.

Friend, don't underestimate the power of your imagination. This is why we continue to remind people to think good thoughts—thoughts of faith, hope, and love (Philippians 4:8). It is only through the sinless life, death, and resurrection of Jesus Christ—the second Adam—that full provision was made for humanity to be restored to a healthy self-image and a life of hope.

If you desire to begin a life of hope and change your image of yourself, then start by changing your thinking. Be careful to whom you listen, as many are full of doubt and have a lack of faith. Be mindful of what you permit to come into your mind through reading, the Internet, social networking, movies, and television. These areas can be full of fear, doubt, cynicism, feelings of hopelessness, and evil information.

A wonderful way to begin developing faith and hope is to meditate on the blessings of God. Through the inspiration of the Holy Spirit, the apostle John wrote, "Beloved, I pray that in all respects you may prosper and be in good health, just as your soul prospers"

(3 John 2 NASB). Here God gives three blessings that He desires for you. He wants you to be prosperous in the spiritual realm, the physical realm, and the material realm. You can:

- Meditate and imagine yourself growing in your spiritual life; think about yourself becoming a person full of faith, courage, and walking in the Spirit.
- Meditate and imagine your career or business becoming successful and prosperous; see the potential of your occupation or the business (or church) that you lead; and permit the Holy Spirit to speak to you about obstacles, as well as creative ideas.
- Meditate and imagine your body being touched by the healing power of God; think about the power of a sound mind, walking in health—both physically and emotionally; specifically ask God for His healing touch.

Begin thinking hopeful thoughts about these truths. Find the time today to get alone with God and talk to Him about these issues, and God will begin to create a renewed self-image and a life of hope within you. Proverbs 16:3 reminds us, "Commit to the LORD whatever you do, and he will establish your plans."

As a follower of Christ, you can have contentment and peace (despite your difficulties) because your faith can produce a settled life of hope for a better today—and future. In the *Anatomy of Hope*, Groopman writes, "To hope under the most extreme circumstances is an act of defiance that ... permits a person to live his life on his own terms. It is part of the human spirit to endure and give a miracle a chance to happen."[3] And the theologian William Barclay said, "The Christian hope is not simply a trembling, hesitant hope that perhaps the promises of God may be true. It is the confident expectation that they cannot be anything else than true."[4]

What you think about has powerful influence on what you

believe. Fill your mind with Scriptures, truths, and information about our wonderful God. Surround yourself with good information, people of faith, and testimonies of God's mighty power. Faith and hope are contagious, so be involved in activities that are healthy. Associate with people of faith and who are full of hope.

Who Are You?

If you don't know who you are, then people will tell you. Who are you—really? If you are living a life full of hopelessness and negative thoughts about yourself, then you will continue to look at yourself in unhealthy ways. Not only must you permit your imagination to change your view of yourself, but you also must use your thinking and effort to solidify your new identity in Christ. You have been transformed, changed, born again. As a child of God, you are not the person you once were. You have been delivered from the kingdom of darkness and transferred into the kingdom of His Son (Colossians 3:13). You are not the person that you were!

For many, it is a great challenge to change their thinking about themselves or to begin to be hopeful. With Christ, all things are possible. By your decision to place your faith in Jesus Christ, you can become a creative, victorious person with a Christlike identity. You can choose to walk away from the negative, doubtful, discouraging thoughts and begin every day with hope.

I (Dr. Cho) was born in Korea during the Japanese occupation. Our conquerors prided themselves on their origins and continually degraded our Korean heritage. Even in our own land, we were considered third-rate citizens. Our entire population suffered from a low national self-concept and overwhelming hopeless thoughts.

When I was a high school student, the Communists invaded my country, an invasion that was to mark the beginning of the Korean War. The war took what little we had left, and my family lived in dire poverty. There were days when we wondered where our next meal would come from—my days and nights were filled with disease and pain.

When I accepted Jesus Christ as my Savior, I immediately knew something was different. I was a child of the King of kings and Lord of lords. I talked to God as if He was my friend. I changed and began to develop a tremendous positive attitude in my thoughts toward my own life. Over the next months and years, I thought of what God could do and began developing my faith that was full of hope. Through faith in Jesus Christ, I rose above my physical, mental, and spiritual poverty and believed in the new identity that God had given me.

Through the Scriptures, I understood that I belonged to Christ and I was a citizen of heaven. In fact, I understood that I was seated in heavenly places. And you are too, if you are a follower of Christ. Even though we live on this earth and in a particular country of origin, we are spiritually seated with Christ. Paul reminds us of this when he writes, "But because of his great love for us, God, who is rich in mercy, made us alive with Christ even when we were dead in transgressions—it is by grace you have been saved. And God raised us up with Christ and seated us with him in the heavenly realms in Christ Jesus" (Ephesians 2:4–6).

Whose Are You?

You are who you are by understanding *whose* you are. In Christ, you are a child of God and are a participant in the divine nature (2 Peter 1:4). With your new identity, you have found that you have a new kind of life, a hopeful life full of God's promises and blessings. Even when suffering we have hope, as we know that we are God's children and He has everything under control. We were born as human beings, created in the image of God as male and female, and have a human nature. As Christians, we are now "children of God" (John 1:12) who are destined to enjoy God's favor and blessings that only He can provide.

If you are basing your life on the temporal, then you will be disillusioned and hope will be hard to find. If you base your new life in Christ and on the eternal, then you will develop a new self-image, confidence, and creativity. You will feel increasingly secure as well. Do not permit anyone or anything to take hope from you. Look to Jesus, for He is full of hope. He knows who you are created to be; the Holy Spirit will speak to you about your new identity in Christ.

What Are Your Dreams?

All of us have dreams and imaginations about what we can become and what we can do. You have dreams, goals, and visions deep inside of you. We are goal-seeking human beings. Many of us have buried our dreams and goals, or we have permitted life's challenges, disappointments, and the words of critical people to steal our dreams. We can overcome those issues and be filled with hope and God's ideas for what we can become and what we can do through His grace.

As people who are created in the image of God, we are wired to be creative, which means we can think of new ways of doing things, helping people, and accomplishing new objectives. Most are not so much motived by their past accomplishments or present environment but by their future goals. What are your goals? Define them. Write them down. In fact, we would encourage you to write down a yearly goal. Concentrate and focus on your goals. And ask the Holy Spirit to speak to your heart about your goals and to inspire them.

You can determine goals for your marriage, career, education, business, and your spiritual life. You also need to always keep in your constant thoughts your most important goal, your eternal goal that is eternal life in heaven through faith in Jesus Christ and life on earth for the glory of God. Even though you become successful in everything you do, if you do not have this ultimate, eternal goal, then you will never have the satisfaction necessary to have a healthy self-image full of hope.

Jürgen Moltmann wrote about where hope is to be found:

> But the ultimate reason for our hope is not to be found at all in what we want, wish for and wait for; the ultimate reason is that we are wanted and wished for and waited for. What is it that awaits us? Does anything await us at all, or are we alone? Whenever we base our hope on trust in the divine mystery, we feel deep down in our hearts: there is someone who is waiting for you, who is hoping for you, who believes in you. We are waited for as his father waits for the prodigal son in the parable. We are accepted and received, as a mother takes her children into her arms and comforts them. God is our last hope because we are God's first love.[5]

God will give you dreams and visions. When you meditate on His Word, pray, and listen, you will hear the still small voice of the Holy Spirit. You will develop new ideas, ways of doing things, and creative thoughts. With these you can begin to set goals and timelines to accomplish the goals God has given you.

What Are You Saying to Yourself?

All of us occasionally have disappointments, but we should never allow disappointments to trigger negative words of resentment and anger, words that lead to self-pity and depression, words that lead to clouded self-concepts, or words that make us feel hopeless.

Jesus understood the power of the spoken word. When He met Simon, He changed his name to Peter. The Hebrew word for *Simon* means "reed." Reeds are swayed by the blowing wind, and the name could point to a person who shifts opinions. *Peter* means "rock," which portrays a picture of a stable person, unbendable and dependable. After Peter received his new name, he was continually reminded that he was stable, strong, and hopeful. It's not surprising that Peter developed into one of the more stable and dependable of all the early apostles.

We can use words that will either help us or harm us. Many are hopeless because of what they say to themselves and what they think about themselves. Words are powerful. The spoken word is the basic material that God used to create the universe. God has given us the ability to speak and express ourselves with words. Much of who we are and what we do are because of what we say to ourselves.

> *Our hope is based on the unfailing promise*
> *of God; why should we not cherish it*
> *confidently and share it boldly?*
> —F. F. Bruce, *The Epistle to the Hebrews*

You can strengthen your hope and your image by focusing on using positive, truthful, and affirming words. Even if you sin, you can ask God for forgiveness, and He will forgive and cleanse you. Don't condemn yourself when you have been forgiven; forgive yourself and begin again. God promises us that "we know that for those who love God all things work together for good, for those who are called according to his purpose" (Romans 8:28 ESV).

Read and memorize God's promises to you, for they will give you strong confidence and hope. You can repeat these promises to yourself and develop an attitude of praise for God's grace. Also, guard what you say about yourself and what you say to others. You are not stupid, unqualified, or unable. You have God's identity as a child of God and are full of the Holy Spirit, forgiven and competent to do all that He has asked you to do. Speak of hope, acts of kindness, encouraging words, words of affirmation, and hope. Discipline yourself today to carefully choose the words that you use to describe yourself.

Where Is Your Faith?

As a person with a new identity in Christ, you can choose to expand into a life of faith, confident in the goals that you have made. Everyone is born with a "measure of faith" (Romans 12:3 KJV). A person who had an idea and had faith in that idea started all of the accomplishments we see in this world. If we haven't had much faith, then we can change and become a person who has a growing faith. We can put our faith into action and have hope that we can grow in our abilities as a person—spiritually, physically, emotionally, and relationally.

On a spiritual level, the best and most lasting results are linked to God. The work of God is faith, for He can create anything in this life. If you put your faith into God's faith, God's faith is going to bring forth God's ability and God's power in you. This will empower you to improve and maintain a life full of hope and a healthy self-image: "The LORD takes pleasure in those who fear him, in those who *hope* in his steadfast love" (Psalm 147:11 ESV).

When I experienced Christ, I had nothing to offer. I was dying, rejected by friends and family, and even the doctor told me I was going to die. The thought that I would be where I am now would have seemed delusional. However, as I grew in my faith, I grew in hope. As I have seen God prove Himself countless times throughout the years, I can now look at goals with great hope. It's all by God's grace. I don't know why God chose me, but before I was born He chose me for such a time as this. It's His grace … and His unique grace is available for you too.

Be full of hope, say good things about yourself, believe God's promises, permit the Holy Spirit to give you a dream, grow in the Word because it will build your faith, and know that God's plans for you are full of hope and a wonderful future: "For I know the plans I have for you, declares the LORD, plans for welfare and not for evil, to give you a future and a hope" (Jeremiah 29:11 ESV).

14

⁓

Prayer:
The Cry of Faith

The language of prayer is forged in the crucible of trouble.
When we can't help ourselves and call for help, when we
don't like where we are and want out, when we don't like
who we are and want a change, we use primal language, and
this language becomes the root language of prayer.

—Eugene Peterson, *Answering God*

On the grounds that surround the main sanctuary (that seats ten thousand people) at Prayer Mountain there are many prayer grottos. I (Dr. Cho) have a prayer grotto where I frequently spend many hours in prayer, meditating on God's Word and listening to the Holy Spirit.

My prayers are not just my words, but much time is spent thinking in prayer, listening, sensing His presence, and communing with the Holy Spirit. Prayer is frequently confusing to some people. It is spiritual, communicating with our God whom we cannot see, and receiving the Holy Spirit's counsel. Prayer is other dimensional, or the "fourth dimension." During these times, I am often inspired by dreams and visions.

You too can receive visions and dreams the Holy Spirit desires to give you. When receiving these inspired thoughts, you can move forward by faith. The Scripture gives us a wonderful example of a person who was without hope and was blind. By faith, this hopeless man decided to enter the fourth dimension. His name was Bartimaeus. The Gospel of Mark tells us the story of a miracle that happened to him, and his life was never the same again:

> And as [Jesus] was leaving Jericho with his disciples and a great crowd, Bartimaeus, a blind beggar, the son of Timaeus, was sitting by the roadside. And when he heard that it was Jesus of Nazareth, he began to cry out and say, "Jesus, Son of David, have mercy on me!" And many rebuked him, telling him to be silent. But he cried out all the more, "Son of David, have mercy on me!" And Jesus stopped and said, "Call him." And they called the blind man, saying to him, "Take heart. Get up; he is calling you." And throwing off his cloak, he sprang up and came to Jesus. And Jesus said to him, "What do you want me to do for you?"
>
> And the blind man said to him, "Rabi, let me recover my sight." And Jesus said to him, "Go your way, your faith has made you well." And immediately he recovered his sight and followed him on the way. (Mark 10:46–52 ESV)

There is a powerful truth that is given with this miracle story: when you feel overwhelmed, hopeless, and do not seem to be able to find answers for your need, know that God understands and will hear your cry of faith.

When you pray, the Holy Spirit frequently makes you aware of His presence. This might happen while you're in a prayer meeting, worship service, or reading and meditating on His Word. You could be in a contemplative mood at work, driving, at your home, or even exercising and sense His presence. His presence could surprise you during the day or the night. During these times (as well as others) you are sensitive to the voice of God and you feel an assurance that Jesus is near. As a child of God, Jesus is near you all the time—you do not need to sense His presence but can be assured by faith that He is listening.

When you sense His presence, seize the moment like Bartimaeus did. Don't delay in asking God to help you. When Bartimaeus heard that Jesus was nearby, he began to shout out, "Jesus, Son of David, have mercy on me!" (Mark 10:47 ESV). Bartimaeus was determined to get Jesus' attention. Some translations use the word "cry out," while others use "shout." Either way, it means the he exclaimed, yelled, screamed, or cried out at the top of his voice to get Jesus' attention.

Bartimaeus desperately wanted to be healed. When he sensed that Jesus didn't notice him when he was walking by, he began shouting all the more. Though he was blind, he desperately pursued Jesus. Notice that he called Jesus the "Son of David!" This was an acknowledgment of faith. Many people said, "Jesus of Nazareth," but this blind man said, "Jesus, Son of David," which is a messianic acknowledgement. He was desperate and he knew that only Jesus could heal him; in fact, his statement acknowledged that Jesus was the Messiah.

When we sense the presence of the Lord near, we need to cry out. When "two or more are gathered," cry out and ask Jesus to help you. On more occasions than I can remember, I have cried out to the Lord. Many of these times I have been alone in my place of prayer or with other people of faith. When we cry out, God hears our heart. We are His children, and just as we do with our child, we immediately pay attention and respond. He always hears our cry. This is why the psalmist could say, "The LORD helps the fallen and lifts up those bent beneath their loads" (Psalm 145:14 NLT).

When we are in desperate situations or our challenges look

hopeless, we resist any fear or apprehension. Even when people mock us or rebuke us for our desperate cry, we choose to tame our fears. We pursue Jesus and avoid people who try to discourage us: "'Be quiet!' many of the people yelled at him. But he only shouted louder, 'Son of David, have mercy on me!'" (Mark 10:48 NLT).

Many times, we are afraid of what others will think or say when we "cry out" in prayer. Why do we care about what others will say? Why are we so concerned about the opinions of others? Our only concern is that we communicate with Jesus and that we hear from Him. He is the Son of God, the one who created us and always hears our voice and understands our thoughts. Proverbs 29:25 says, "Fearing people is a dangerous trap, but whoever trusts in the LORD is kept safe."

Don't let fear of looking foolish, other people's opinions, or circumstances hold you back. Cry out to God. If you feel more comfortable doing this in a place where you are alone, then find that place. Don't let people's criticism (or satan's) keep you from your step of faith. When we are asking for a miracle, wisdom, a divine idea, financial help, or healing, we must announce our faith and specifically give our request to God:

"What do you want me to do for you?" Jesus asked him.
The blind man said, "Rabbi, I want to see." (Mark 10:51)

What is your need today? Jesus knows what you are going to request before you say the words—and He knows the desires of your heart. When we cry out to Jesus and express our concern or discuss our need with Him, it is important to be specific.

My Cry Was Specific

When we were building on Yoido Island, we ran out of funds. The oil shock broke out in the Middle East, and the value of our currency fell against the dollar. The price of building materials rose and many of our members lost their jobs. This led to a decrease in offerings and our ability to receive a loan from a bank. The pressure of debt came to the climax. Additionally, we had an architectural technique problem that contributed to the interruption of the construction. I didn't know what to do, and it seemed that we were in a perfect storm coming from all directions. There was nowhere to turn.

I cried out to the Lord, and many times fell on the cement floor of the basement of the sanctuary, and prayed for the *specific needs*—to build the sanctuary. Only the framework was completed at the time. Through a series of miracles, the Saving the Church Movement began. Hundreds of our church members fasted and desperately prayed every evening in the basement. As a result, the sanctuary was finally built. And after the sanctuary was built, Prayer Mountain was built, which has been a tremendous contribution to the church's revival.

---

*"Will not God bring about justice for
his chosen ones, who cry to him day and night?
Will he keep putting them off?"*
—Luke 18:7

When you sense that you have the answer, or feel an assurance that God has heard your prayer, then receive God's grace. Take the step and begin to move by faith in the direction that will reach your goal or dream: "'Go,' said Jesus, 'your faith has healed you.' Immediately [the blind man] received his sight and followed Jesus along the road" (Mark 10:52).

Walk away with the answer. The answer could be a vision, a dream, a detailed plan, specific instructions, or a deep sense of assurance. Answers from God come in obvious ways—"Instantly the blind man could see!"—or answers can come in ways of assurance that our prayer has been heard and the answer is on the way (Daniel 10:12). With that assurance, we can sense a unique peace that God will work it out. When we sense this peace, we hold steady in our faith and trust Him.

Today, Jesus stands ready to hear your cry and
to answer prayer for you. He is interested in every detail
of your life. He knows you better than you know yourself.
—Kathryn Kuhlman

There have been countless times when I knew that God heard my prayer—I felt assurance and peace. Even though I did not know the details, or the timing, I knew that God's timing would be perfect. When that time came, the answer would be there. When we sense that we have the answer, or that the miracle is on its way, we take the next step by faith.

We continually remind ourselves that the righteous walk by faith. Faith is a necessary component to receiving answers to prayer, stepping out toward the dream God has given us, or believing the Holy Spirit when He gives us divine thoughts, goals, truths by which to live, or the miracle that we need.

When we step out, we have evaluated the situation, we have moved to a higher level of evaluation and trust. During these times, we might consult with a wise counselor, a godly person who knows how to pray and touch God. The Scripture tells us in the abundance of counselors, plans succeed (Proverbs 15:22). God's Word reminds us to consider the costs. Jesus asks:

"Suppose one of you wants to build a tower. Won't you first sit down and estimate the cost to see if you have enough money to complete it? For if you lay the foundation and are not able to finish it, everyone who sees it will ridicule you, saying, 'This person began to build and wasn't able to finish.'

Or suppose a king is about to go to war against another king. Won't he first sit down and consider whether he is able with ten thousand men to oppose the one coming against him with twenty thousand?" (Luke 14:28–31)

When you have prayed, studied the Scriptures to ensure that your goal is biblical, listened to the wise advice of godly people, and considered the cost (evaluated the time, effort, expenses, etc.), take the step of faith in your business, your ministry, the needs of your family, and your life goals. James 2:14 asks us, "What's the use of saying you have faith if you don't prove it by your actions?" You might say, "This is so difficult. How can I do this when I don't actually see the answer?"

When I received the US Army tent that became the beginning of our church, I could not see anyone except my future mother-in-law and her daughters, one of which became my wonderful wife. At that time, I did not know that the beginning of healing miracles would be three deaf people; I didn't see (with my physical eyes) the hundreds of people who would come to that location and find Jesus. Many were healed and filled with the Holy Spirit. I did not physically see it, but *I sensed God's assurance* to step out in faith and believe.

In our first building, I did not anticipate parking problems, or that the building would become so full of needy people (multiple times a week) that we would need to move and build a larger building. But I *sensed in my heart* that the Lord would bring tens of thousands to the church who would find the answers to life. Their experience with Christ was like a magnet that drew people to the Lord.

In our Yoido church, I did not see with my physical eyes the hundreds of thousands of people who would come, that physical miracles, financial miracles, and powerful moves of the Holy Spirit would happen. But *by faith and assurance, I knew* it would happen. This church has impacted millions, God has touched South Korea, and many nations have been influenced by the example (and faith) of the people in our church.

We cry out to God, tame our fear, specifically request our needs, and with God's assurance we receive it (with thanksgiving and grace), and step out in faith. Be encouraged that you are a child of God. He always hears you. His timing is always perfect. God will give you His assurance, and by faith, along with God's grace, you can do it.

David and Moses Cried Out to God

David was an anointed leader who had been chosen to be the king. Because of Saul's jealousy and fear of David becoming king, Saul wanted him dead. Repeatedly, Saul tried to determine where David was at; he wanted to find him and eliminate him (1 Samuel 23). Like many of us would, David frequently cried out to God. For example, at one time he prayed:

> I cry aloud to the LORD;
>> I lift up my voice to the LORD for mercy.
> I pour out before him my complaint;
>> before him I tell my trouble. (Psalm 142:1)

And Exodus 15:25 tells us, "Then Moses cried out to the LORD, and the LORD showed him a piece of wood. He threw it into the water, and the water became fit to drink." Matthew Henry describes this situation in this way:

> In the wilderness of Shur the Israelites had no water. At Marah they had water, but it was bitter; so that they could

not drink it. God can make bitter to us that from which we promise ourselves most, and often does so in the wilderness of this world, that our wants, and disappointments in the creature, may drive us to the Creator, in whose favor alone true comfort is to be had. In this distress the people fretted, and quarreled with Moses. Hypocrites may show high affections, and appear earnest in religious exercises, but in the time of temptation they fall away. Even true believers, in seasons of sharp trial, will be tempted to fret, distrust, and murmur. But in every trial we should cast our care upon the Lord, and pour out our hearts before him. We shall then find that a submissive will, a peaceful conscience, and the comforts of the Holy Ghost, will render the bitterest trial tolerable, yea, pleasant. Moses did what the people had neglected to do; he cried unto the Lord. And God provided graciously for them. He directed Moses to a tree, which he cast into the waters, when, at once, they were made sweet. Some make this tree typical of the cross of Christ, which sweetens the bitter waters of affliction to all the faithful, and enables them to rejoice in tribulation. But a rebellious Israelite shall fare no better than a rebellious Egyptian. The threatening is implied only the promise is expressed. God is the great Physician. If we are kept well, it is he that keeps us; if we are made well, it is he that recovers us. He is our life and the length of our days. Let us not forget that we are kept from destruction, and delivered from our enemies, to be the Lord's servants. At Elim they had good water, and enough of it. Though God may, for a time, order his people to encamp by the bitter waters of Marah that shall not always be their lot. Let us not faint at tribulations.[1]

Bill Gothard writes that "after knowing the Lord Jesus Christ and teaching and studying His Word for many years, it was only recently that I made what was for me a life-changing discovery. I saw that the Bible makes a distinction between 'prayer' and 'crying out to God.'"[2] I (Dr. Cho) have noticed that, at times, God has allowed circumstances to arise that seem to have no solution, and then do nothing to remove the problem—until I cry out. And not one second sooner!

Each situation seems so hopeless, and sometimes a cry seems futile. Yet this is precisely the setting God wants so He can demonstrate His loving care and His powerful hand of protection. Sometimes a cry will bring freedom from emotional bondage; in other cases, God will provide healing from a disease, help in a moment of grave danger, or clear direction in a season of deep perplexity. In every circumstance, however, the need to cry out is a humbling reminder of our total inability to accomplish anything significant for God. The result is a wonderful demonstration of His supernatural power to achieve all that is needed.

Become Desperate for God

God's promise to the prophet so long ago is just as true for us in these uncertain days of the twenty-first century: "Call to me and I will answer you and tell you great and unsearchable things you do not know" (Jeremiah 33:3). If we don't pray, then little will happen. Your prayer is forth dimensional—as you say words to God that you cannot see, He will hear you as you cry out, or in the consistency of your specific prayers.

Many leaders are concerned about congregations that have little prayer. Erwin Lutzer, longtime pastor of Chicago's Moody Church, observes: "I find it very interesting that even though as a church generally we complain about the present darkness, we still are not desperate enough to sincerely pray and call congregations to pray. If the darkness is as bad as we believe it is morally and spiritually, why is it that we still do not pray?"[3]

Yoido Full Gospel Church has always—and I mean always— made prayer a primary mandate. We have overnight prayer meetings and spontaneous prayer times. In fact, our development of Prayer Mountain is a constant reminder that we must pray continually. The people of the church understand this.

Many are preoccupied with the circumstances that surround them. It seems harder today than in past generations to get people to attend prayer meetings, or to develop a disciplined prayer life. When I talk to many of my friends from other locations around the world, I frequently ask them about their personal prayer time and how they focus on this discipline. I speak to business and political leaders and people from all walks of life and try to sense how much they depend on God and make prayer a consistent practice in their lives. I frequently hear that prayer meetings are not happening as frequently, many times of prayer have degenerated into gossip sessions, or one person has dominated the meeting with long prayers.

Decision Magazine writer Bob Paulson writes, "Is any other practice so universally extolled yet so often left undone by Christians? And in an age when true followers of Christ increasingly are marginalized, mocked and despised, can we continue to act as if we don't need to cry out for God's help?"[4] And Billy Graham reminds us that "prayer is spiritual communication between man and God, a two-way relationship in which man should not only talk to God but also listen to Him. Prayer to God is like a child's conversation with his father. It is natural for a child to ask his father for the things he needs."[5]

You are no different from the blind person, the desperate person, and the typical human being who needs God's help. The Scripture gives us this truth because God wants us to be reminded that in our desperation we can pursue Jesus, cry out to Him, and be persistent in our requests for the miracle or healing that we need. You are His child; He created you in His image. You are forgiven, free from accusation, and are uniquely gifted. As a mother always hears the quiet whimpering of her baby in the night, so Jesus always hears your heart, knows your desperate thoughts, and hears your cry of faith.

15

✑

Be Confident
in Your Faith

St. Augustine wrote that our hearts are restless until
they find their rest in Him. In a day when many notable
Christian leaders are trying to find a way to make the
Gospel relevant, I propose that authentic Christianity is
already relevant. Christianity meets the deepest needs
of the human heart—to know God and not just about Him;
to know Jesus as Friend and Brother; to experience the
power of His Spirit and resurrection in living as new
creations, healed of all the evil that holds us down.
—Francis MacNutt, *The Nearly Perfect Crime*

My aim is to know him, to experience the
power of his resurrection, to share in his sufferings,
and to be like him in his death.
—Philippians 3:10 NET

Not long ago the British Broadcasting Company (BBC) came
to Korea to do a program. When interviewing me (Dr. Cho),
the reporter asked, "Why is it that the European Christian church
is becoming smaller and smaller while the church in Korea is pros-

pering? Why are the churches in the European countries empty and no one comes, but in Korea the church is filled in the morning, filled in the afternoon, and filled in the evening and the people in the church are growing spiritually?" I listened and prayed for God to give me wisdom to answer his question. Then he went on and said, "If you give a long answer, the people will turn off the television. So keep your answer short."

I sensed a desire from him to know the answer to his somewhat complicated question. So I said, "The reason many of the churches in England and other European countries are shrinking is because many of the ministers in those countries have been overeducated. They are preaching theology. They are preaching philosophy. They are preaching culture. They are preaching religion. To many of them, Jesus has become a historical person who lived a long time ago. Many believe that the Holy Spirit's movement ended with the book of Acts. They do not believe that miracles could happen today. They believe in a God of history, and they think the Bible is a historical book. They quote it as a formality."

In saying that, please understand that we (Dr. Cho and Wayde) pray for Europe, America, and many other Western countries. If it weren't for the wonderful missionaries that the Assemblies of God sent to the nations, neither of us would have the faith that we have. We owe a great debt to the dedicated, sacrificial, and encouraging work of US missionaries and for the tremendous ministries of the nineteenth and twentieth centuries that are the roots of our doctrines.

Faith is not something you have to get.
It's something that you, as a born-again child of God,
already have. Act on it by releasing it to God.
That's when your healing starts.
—Oral Roberts

There is a popular opinion that the miracles, signs, and wonders, and the anointed men and women whom we read about in the book of Acts are just part of the past. These people say that the miracles of Acts are no longer available for us today, and that the miracles of the Bible can be humanly explained. This is a lie from the enemy. The facts are that miracles, signs, and wonders are very much part of the tremendous move of God—globally. Francis MacNutt explains:

> Something else is happening on a worldwide scale. Pentecostal Christians have, in the last hundred years, rediscovered the power of the Holy Spirit, together with the willingness of God to heal and free His people. They do not see healing as something rare and reserved to a special class of people. They are returning to the model of the early Church, the deepest tradition: "Everyone gets to play." These Pentecostal-evangelical-charismatic churches are growing at an explosive rate.[1]

Two Kinds of Gospel

There are two kinds of gospels: one is of humans and the other is the gospel of Jesus Christ, which is inspired by the Holy Spirit. Some people interpret the gospel from a humanistic viewpoint and think that Jesus was only a human being who lived some two thousand years ago. Others believe that Jesus was only a historic figure, or perhaps one of the many ways to have eternal life.

There are many denominational groups that most certainly believe in Jesus our resurrected Lord; however, they believe that the miracles, signs, and wonders were discontinued when the Acts of the Apostles ended. The Bible explains Jesus: He is the only way of salvation and eternal life (John 14:6); He is our salvation because He paid the price for all our sins on the cross; and from the first-century church till today, signs, wonders, miracles, and the wonderful moving of the Holy Spirit have been present.

The truth that is found in Jesus Christ is under attack from the enemy. He has inspired so-called scholars to bring doubt into the minds of many. Some laugh at those who believe in a miracle-working God. They are cynical, unbelieving, and question the truth. Like a poison that can invade a person's body, they are teachers of doubt, unbelief, and compromise. We are living in a time when the gospel and miracles of the Bible are under attack like never before.

The enemy will attack your faith and determination to believe the truths found in the Scripture. It is important to know the strategy of the enemy. When you understand the many ways that he will try to destroy your faith, then you can pray for God's protection and be assured that the enemy cannot remove God's blessings from your life and that you belong to Jesus. C. S. Lewis said, "I believe in Christianity as I believe that the Sun has risen, not only because I see it, but because by it I see everything else."[2]

For God so loved the world, that he gave his only begotten Son, that whosoever believeth in him should not perish, but have everlasting life.

—John 3:16 KJV

We can humbly come to Jesus and, by faith, believe that He died for us and that He physically rose from the dead. Then we confess with our words that He is Lord, and we will have the greatest miracle happen to us—we will immediately become born again (Romans 10:9–10). At that moment, we have become a temple of the Holy Spirit (1 Corinthians 3:16). He invades our lives. The Bible tells us that we will receive peace and purpose in Jesus Christ, and the Holy Spirit will teach us and guide us as we live our lives (John 14–16).

For you know the grace of our Lord Jesus Christ,
that though he was rich, yet for your sake he became
poor, so that you by his poverty might become rich.
—2 Corinthians 8:9

Redeemed from the Curse of the Law

Paul wrote, "Christ redeemed us from the curse of the law by becoming a curse for us. … He redeemed us in order that the blessing given to Abraham might come to the Gentiles through Christ Jesus, so that by faith we might receive the promise of the Spirit (Galatians 3:13–14).

When Jesus comes into your life, He gives freedom. He will make you free on the inside, and free from the prison of the world. The children of Adam (humans) were prisoners of the devil, but through the cross of Calvary Jesus took away that bondage. The devil has lost his teeth—they are broken because of the blood of Jesus. Jesus took away all the weapons of the enemy. He will falsely accuse you, try to intimidate and frighten you, and develop temptations that will cause you to lose faith or even fall. Please understand that the devil will do all that he can to stop you in your faith walk; however, because of what Jesus did for you, the enemy cannot harm you (1 John 5:18).

The Bible declares that we who were once prisoners of the devil are now free: "You have been set free from sin and have become slaves to righteousness" (Romans 6:18). And again, "He has delivered us from the domain of darkness and transferred us to the kingdom of his beloved Son" (Colossians 1:13 ESV). Although we were in prisons of bondage, hatred, sin, and fear, we are now free to be joyful, loving people who are destined to live righteous lives in Christ. We *were* prisoners of worry, anxiety, discouragement, despair, and frustration, but we are now healed by the grace of Jesus Christ. The Holy Spirit who resides in us will continually remind us of all that Jesus has done (John 14:26). Once you have become a Christian, you are no longer held in prison by these things. You have been set free by the cross of Christ.

Are you imprisoned by hatred toward others who have hurt or rejected you? Has someone abused you? Through the blood of Jesus Christ, you can become free and strong. No matter who you are or what position you have, the enemy of your soul will endeavor to trap or attack you. The Scripture speaks of the snares, traps, and deceptions of the enemy. He does not want you to walk in truth and freedom; he creates temptations and hunts down "the precious life" (Proverbs 6:26).

The devil follows us around trying to tempt and test us with evil and sin. This causes pain, such as depression, addictions, immorality, unfulfilled dreams, and discouragement. The devil wants to occupy our hearts and minds. He wants to steal, kill, and destroy. He wants to disturb and destroy our families. Jesus said that the devil "was a murderer from the beginning, and does not stand in the truth because there is no truth in him. Whenever he speaks a lie, he speaks from his own nature, for he is a liar and the father of lies" (John 8:44 NASB).

Jesus came to destroy the work of the enemy (1 John 3:8; Hebrews 2:14). As you walk with Christ, He will destroy every work the enemy has brought into your life. You are equipped and armed with the name of Jesus. In Him, you have the capability to overcome the devil.

The Bible tells us, "Submit yourselves therefore to God. Resist the devil, and he will flee from you" (James 4:7 ESV). Because God is a good God, He can change your life and make it more abundant. When Jesus comes into your life, something good will happen to you. Jesus is the same yesterday, today, and forever; what He did for all the incredible people of faith in the Bible He can do for you too. You can trust Jesus to enable you to get rid of all your discouragement, insecurities, feelings of failure, and bondage to life-controlling habits. He can set you free.

Be filled with the Holy Spirit today. Live in the freedom that Jesus has provided for you. The Holy Spirit will remind you of His truths and help you.

Open to God's Promises

When Christ comes into our lives, we become open to the wonderful promises of God and to His spiritual truths. Jesus is the Light of the World. As we walk in the Spirit, we can see spiritual truths. The most important of all God's revelations is that Jesus Christ is the only Son of God, He is alive, and whoever believes in Him shall not perish but have eternal life (John 3:16).

We can be free from anxiety, worry, fear, and a sense of rejection. The Holy Spirit will help us understand and receive His blessings that will enable us to prosper in all things, even as our souls prosper. When you understand this truth, then you will be able to have dominion over your physical world. John prayed, "Beloved, I pray that in all respects you may prosper and be in good health, just as your soul prospers" (3 John 2 NASB).

The Bible tells us that Jesus will release the oppressed: "God anointed Jesus of Nazareth with the Holy Spirit and with power. He went about doing good and healing all who were oppressed by the devil, for God was with him" (Acts 10:38 ESV). Without Christ, humanity is oppressed and bound with the stresses of life. This is not the life that God has for you. Your Creator desires that you have an abundant and fulfilled life (John 10:10).

The Bible tells us that Jesus came to proclaim the year of the Lord. After the sins of Adam and Eve in the garden of Eden, the world has become more and more chaotic, confused, and influenced by satan. After the fall, people started getting into an age of consciousness. The people lived under their own consciences. When Moses came, the law was given, but the people were struggling and unable to obey it.

When Jesus died on the cross, He paid the entire price for our sins. He died for us and rose again, and now when we accept Him as our Savior, we become free and liberated. It is then that we enter the dispensation of the church, which is a dispensation of grace. This is the time when faith becomes most important. This time of grace is not something you have to work for or become perfect to receive; it is a gift, a special present from the Lord.

The law said we had to do certain things, and we had to do a long list of laws that were impossible to fulfill. We cannot earn or buy salvation. It is a gift from God that comes only because of the grace of God. By faith we believe that Jesus paid the price for our redemption on the cross, and gave us justification with forgiveness and salvation. Paul confidently declared, "Sin will have no dominion over you, since you are not under the law but under grace" (Romans 6:14 ESV).

Boldness to Declare Good News

Jesus lived for approximately thirty-three years, which ended with His death, burial, and resurrection. From the day of Pentecost, when the Holy Spirit was poured out on the 120 believers in the upper room (Acts 2:4), the Holy Spirit has powerfully moved through believers to advance the kingdom throughout the world. The Holy Spirit established the church and helps us evangelize this world with the good news of Jesus.

The Bible tells us to declare the good news. It is the Holy Spirit who gives us eternal life. If you are lost and empty, God wants to give you purpose and meaning. If you are poor or oppressed, God wants to give you prosperity and freedom. Jesus is alive today, and

He loves you. Jesus tells us, "Come to me, all who labor and are heavy laden, and I will give you rest" (Matthew 11:28 ESV). Jesus carried the cross to Calvary, shed His blood, and died for us. He loved us even when we did not love Him. We can now receive freedom and healing and blessings; we can now receive eternal life and the Holy Spirit.

We don't have to live a life of bondage any longer. If we are in despair, we can be helped. Through Jesus, we have love, hope, and peace. Jesus wants to give us prosperity. He not only gives us life, but life more abundantly. People of the world cannot see and cannot hear because they are living in the flesh. We only see with spiritual eyes if we are born again. So He gives us this new spiritual life through the Holy Spirit. We can understand the moving of the Holy Spirit and we can know God's purpose in our lives. This gives us a hope that most do not understand, a life full of hope.

Despair is the beginning of death, but in Christ we can have confidence. God is for you. The devil gives us despair, but God wants to fill us with anticipation of His goodness and His possibilities. Tomorrow will be better than today. The day after that will be even better. Our prayer life will get better and better. The devil wants to put us down, but we are not going to be affected by that. From Jesus we receive power and authority to resist and defeat the devil, casting him out in the name of Jesus (Mark 16:17; Acts 16:18).

Be Confident

The Holy Spirit will help us gain confidence. He is with us eternally. He is our Comforter. He is our Helper. He is our Counselor. He gives us inspiration and informs us about the future. He is the person who wants to be with us. The Spirit is with us today, so acknowledge Him. Welcome and depend on the Holy Spirit, then you can have this amazing grace from God. You will have the best time of your life without living a life of despair.

We are *not* living in an age of the law. We are living in a period of grace. Because of the cross of Calvary, we are living in His grace where we can have faith. We don't have to be lost. We can live a life of prosperity and fulfillment. The Bible says we need faith and we need to fight for the kingdom of God. Let us resist the devil and break through; Jesus will help us do this. We will experience miracles when we do this. We need to carry the freedom of Christ with us. We can enjoy eternal life. We can enjoy prosperity in all we do. Through the power of Jesus, we will live an effective life. So we can sing loudly,

> "O death, where is your victory?
>   O death, where is your sting?"
>   The sting of death is sin, and the power of sin is the law.
> But thanks be to God,
>   who gives us the victory through our Lord Jesus Christ.
> (1 Corinthians 15:56–57 ESV)

We can be an instrument of God and have victory in our daily lives. The Bible tells us that the kingdom of God is neither here nor there, but it is in the midst of us. Even though the whole world is torn apart, we cannot be moved. We do not have to be in despair or depressed because the kingdom of God is with us. No matter what kind of persecution comes upon us, we are not afraid because the kingdom of God is with us.

With each step of faith that I (Dr. Cho) have taken in our church and in my personal life, I have had overwhelming feelings of despair and the enemy has haunted my thinking with statements like, "What if this doesn't work?" and "You are foolish to attempt this—people will mock you for your foolishness." During each of these times, I have become fearful and had thoughts of discontinuing and giving up. I, too, have needed to say, "Yonggi, resist the devil and trust Jesus. Let the wonderful Holy Spirit help me and provide the miracles that I need." In doing that, my confidence has grown and the assurance has developed in my heart and mind.

Be confident, for Jesus will never, never, never leave you or forsake you. He has given the precious Holy Spirit to guide you, counsel you, warn you, teach you, and open the doors that you need to have opened. Stand today—on your faith. "Dear friends, although I was very eager to write to you about the salvation we share, I felt compelled to write and urge you to contend for the faith that was once for all entrusted to God's holy people" (Jude 3). Be confident in the faith God has given you.

16

*

Faith, Power, and Impartation

"You will receive power when the Holy Spirit has come upon
you, and you will be my witnesses in Jerusalem and in all
Judea and Samaria, and to the end of the earth."
—Acts 1:8 ESV

Ever present on my mind is the miraculous healing that I (Dr.
Cho) received along with the manifestation of the Lord that
appeared to me in my small room. When I was dying, I thought
that room would be the final place I would live. So many miraculous things happened surrounding that event: the girl who wouldn't
give up in her determination to convince me to give my life to
Christ, the presence of Jesus, the healing I sensed was happening,
and the missionaries who happened to be nearby who encouraged
me and brought me wise counsel. These were all part of my beginning experiences that impacted me and gave me a strong sense of
God's calling on my life.

Deep inside, I knew God had selected me to be a leader in His
kingdom. And looking back, I see His wonderful grace. All that I am
is because of the grace of Jesus Christ. His forgiveness, anointing,

charismatic gifts, healing power, and talents, along with my dear family, my ministry, and the baptism in the Holy Spirit, are all God's grace.

"I baptize you with water for repentance,
but he who is coming after me is mightier than I,
whose sandals I am not worthy to carry. He will
baptize you with the Holy Spirit and fire."

—Matthew 3:11 ESV

After I began to understand what had happened to me, I sought further confirmation from the Bible that I had been transformed and transferred to another kingdom, "the kingdom of His beloved Son" (Colossians 1:13 NASB). Missionaries became part of my early experience as they taught me from the Scriptures, encouraging and explaining to me the Bible. Through their teaching and my study, I understood that I was now a Christ-follower, a child of God. I also understood that the baptism with the Holy Spirit would empower me and I could have faith to believe for more.

Jesus explained all of this to His disciples on the day before He was crucified. He wanted them to understand that He was physically leaving them, but it would be better for them because the Holy Spirit would then infill them. This infilling would be a unique supernatural power that would bring enablement to become global witnesses—the miraculous power and presence of God would be part of their ministry.

For the first three hundred years of church history, healings, miracles, deliverances, and the advance of Christianity flourished. For hundreds of years after that, cynicism, liberal teaching, and countless false doctrines and extra-biblical teachings came to the church. Today we need to be reminded of this empowerment that Jesus taught the disciples.

Baptism in the Holy Spirit

Faith to believe in miracles is greatly enhanced by the baptism in the Holy Spirit. When we read the Gospels, we can't miss the fact that Jesus healed the sick, cast out demons, and raised the dead. Jesus was greatly concerned that the disciples knew He had not abandoned them but in fact gave them a more powerful, fulfilling life as they experienced the Holy Spirit. There is no question that He deeply desired that the early apostles would experience the infilling of the Holy Spirit.

When Jesus attended the Feast of Tabernacles, He saw desperate, needy people. He sensed their inner longing for spiritual truth:

> On the last day of the feast, the great day, Jesus stood up and cried out, "If anyone thirsts, let him come to me and drink. Whoever believes in me, as the Scripture has said, 'Out of his heart will flow rivers of living water.'" Now this he said about the Spirit, whom those who believed in him were to receive, for as yet the Spirit had not been given, because Jesus was not yet glorified. (John 7:37–39 ESV)

In the last conversation with Jesus' disciples, before His crucifixion (John 13–17), Jesus promised to send the Holy Spirit to them (and all future disciples) after His physical departure. They were upset about this saying. They had grown to depend on Him, listened to Him, and experienced some of the miracles He had done. Jesus was always there teaching, demonstrating, counseling, and showing them how to help and heal people. They sensed His peace and anointing, and they loved His presence. They couldn't imagine not having Him physically with them. What would they do? They had left everything to follow and learn from Him; in fact, they were dependent on the physical Jesus.

Knowing they were disappointed with the thought of His departure, Jesus encouraged them by telling them it would be better that He physically leave them. He explained that when He departed, He would come to them in a way that (at that time) they did not understand. He explained: "Nevertheless, I tell you the truth: it is to your advantage that I go away, for if I do not go away, the Helper will not come to you. But if I go, I will send him to you" (John 16:7 ESV).

This is a powerful truth full of revelation that, with the help of the Holy Spirit, they could understand. Jesus promised that when He was physically gone from this earth, He would be with them (and us) in a more impactful way. This involved the Holy Spirit being with them wherever they individually went, and He would constantly remind them of Jesus' teachings as well as other truths, information about the future, and what to do in the circumstances they faced. His power would reside within them as they walked in the Spirit.

These were only hopeful words. At the time, they did not know what this meant or how it would happen. Jesus would come with the Father and the Holy Spirit and live within them (and us). This would be better than walking and talking and being with Jesus physically—or watching Him as He performed miracles and healed the sick. The disciples, much like us, simply could not comprehend the idea that it would be better for them when He departed.

The disciples had developed a dying trust in His words. Their minds could not appreciate what He was saying. How would this ever be? Jesus said it, so it must be true. Their minds and imaginations began to actively think about what would happen to them after He was gone. With the death of Jesus, confusion became present in their lives.

Hours before His death, Jesus instructed the disciples that when the Holy Spirit began to live within them, then they would be led into all truth:

"I still have many things to say to you, but you cannot bear them now. When the Spirit of truth comes, he will guide you into all the truth, for he will not speak on his own authority, but whatever he hears he will speak, and he will declare to you the things that are to come." (John 16:12–13 ESV)

At His death and burial, the disciples were in shock. They felt hopeless and did not know what to do. They met, talked, and wondered what was going to happen. Some began returning to their previous occupations—surely there was anticipation about how His promises, teachings, and presence would be unfolded. The brief time after His death was full of questions—anxiety and hesitation—about what they would do. They needed to trust His words, they needed to have faith that what He said would happen.

The resurrected Jesus visited them, like He had promised, and reminded them of the fact that they would receive the Holy Spirit. He reminded them of what He had been teaching them, and He continued to talk about the kingdom of God and how they were to wait for "the promise." Seeing the resurrected Lord was amazing and brought these early church leaders a deep assurance that is beyond description.

After Jesus' resurrection and before His ascension, Luke writes, "[Jesus] presented himself to them and gave many convincing proofs that he was alive. He appeared to them over a period of forty days and spoke about the kingdom of God" (Acts 1:3). For forty days, He taught them about the kingdom of God, reminding them of His teachings and preparing them for the incredible impact they would have as God's kingdom powerfully advanced. However, to do this, they would need the power of the Holy Spirit.

While staying with them, Jesus instructed them not to depart from Jerusalem, but to wait for the promise of the Father, which, He said, "you heard from me; for John baptized with water, but you will be baptized with the Holy Spirit not many days from now" (Acts 1:4–5 ESV). The disciples intimately knew Jesus and now were witnesses of His resurrection.

By faith they anticipated the promise. They now thought, *This must be true—the Holy Spirit will fill us, be with us, speak to us; as a result, we will have power to do what Jesus taught us to do.* Doubt had turned into belief—even anticipation—and a sense that it was going to happen. But how? Jesus said, "You will receive power when the Holy Spirit has come upon you, and you will be my witnesses in Jerusalem and in all Judea and Samaria, and to the end of the earth" (Acts 1:8 ESV).

The Promise

The disciples followed Jesus' instructions and prayed in the upper room for ten days after His ascension.[1] Many others were with them—the Bible says about 120 people were gathered together, including Jesus' mother and brothers. Peter seemed to become the leader as he conducted the first business meeting to determine who would replace Judas (Acts 2:15–26). The 120 continued to pray and wait with anticipation, and then what they could not imagine happened! Luke writes, "And they were all filled with the Holy Spirit and began to speak in other tongues as the Spirit gave them utterance" (Acts 2:4 ESV).

Without a storm, there was a rush of a mighty wind; without a fire, they saw tongues of fire descending on everyone; and without language training, they spoke in languages they did not know. The infilling of the Holy Spirit was happening, what Jesus had promised was coming to pass. With this experience they no longer wondered how it would all happen. They suddenly knew.

The 120 believers were baptized with the Holy Spirit. Outside the upper room, people heard the excitement and different languages being spoken. The crowd grew and Peter felt the Holy

Spirit's encouragement and sensed His anointing and the powerful impulse to tell the curious people what was happening. He preached his first sermon to thousands that day, and three thousand people were saved and received the infilling of the Holy Spirit. The disciples believed Jesus—they waited with anticipation—and the words of Jesus became a reality. And so they began to tell the world about Jesus, the resurrected Christ!

Much more than mere words, they now had an experience. With that, they began to understand how it would be better for them when their precious Friend and Lord departed and the Holy Spirit filled them. They also knew that He was always with them (Hebrews 13:5). In his inspired sermon, Peter explained what was going on by quoting the prophet Joel's words from hundreds of years before:

> "And in the last days it shall be, God declares,
> that I will pour out my Spirit on all flesh,
> and your sons and your daughters shall prophesy,
> and your young men shall see visions,
> and your old men shall dream dreams;
> even on my male servants and female servants
> in those days I will pour out my Spirit, and they shall prophesy."
> (Acts 2:17–18 ESV)

Joel gave this remarkable prophecy that all of God's family (the church) would be equal—because God is no respecter of persons—and God would pour out His Spirit on every hungry believer. The poor, broken, wounded—all races and nationalities—those at the time who were considered the least in society (women, slaves, and young people) would be given this supernatural blessing and power. When Joel gave this prophecy, it seemed impossible. But now it was happening.

Empowerment

Right after the outpouring of God's Spirit on the day of Pentecost (Acts 2) and the infilling of thousands of people, Peter and John deeply sensed the power of God, a dynamic infilling that greatly encouraged their faith. They sensed boldness within that gave them courage, a deep sense of assurance, and they believed for the miraculous. As they were walking to the temple to pray at about three in the afternoon, they saw a crippled beggar. He wanted money, but Peter knew he could give him something better than what money could buy:

> Peter said, "I have no silver and gold, but what I do have I give to you. In the name of Jesus Christ of Nazareth, rise up and walk!" And he took him by the right hand and raised him up, and immediately his feet and ankles were made strong. And leaping up he stood and began to walk, and entered the temple with them, walking and leaping and praising God. (Acts 3:6–8 ESV)

Peter's name had been changed from *Simon*—the reed that changes according to the blowing of the wind—to *Peter* "the rock," which means stable, solid, and secure. He had unmovable faith! John was now full of supernatural faith, hope, and love. He agreed with Peter's prayer and it happened. The beggar was healed!

Where Are We Today?

In much of the global church today, there is a lack of faith. There are churches, communities, and even countries where there are evidences of great faith where the miraculous happens and the baptism with the Holy Spirit is proclaimed without hesitation. However, some leaders, churches, and denominations doubt this experience or are afraid to proclaim it. Doctrinally, they might believe that the miraculous can still happen—healings can occur and people can receive the gifts of the Holy Spirit (1 Corinthians 12); however, in their experiences, seldom does the miraculous happen or do people receive this baptism in the Holy Spirit.

Why is this? Perhaps it is doubt, fear of being wrong, or a lack of hunger for God. They may also believe that the charismatic gifts ended with the early apostles. It could be that a pastor is concerned that the people will be excessive or that the people they serve will think they are over the edge and believe he or she is being extreme. Many do not know what to say when people are not healed when they pray, so they decide not to pray for miracles or healing at all. These ideas and questions are full of doubt. We pray by faith, believing that the Holy Spirit will empower us and use us, just as He did with the early church.

The enemy does not want this experience to happen to believers, because when we receive this experience we become powerful, bold, and a greater witness. We become a serious threat to his dark kingdom. This demonic kingdom will do everything it can to discourage you, to bring doubt into your mind, and persuade you to not pray by faith, or trust the power of Holy Spirit within you.

Do not yield to doubt. Believe and trust God to use you with the charismatic gifts. Be filled with the Holy Spirit, listen to His voice from within, and ask Him to guide you to believe in the miraculous. As you talk to people about how to make Jesus the Lord of their lives, the miracle of salvation happens. Charismatic miracles can happen too—people can be healed both physically and mentally, and spiritually delivered. It is most exciting to see God's power and grace demonstrated in a wounded and confused person's life.

Our individual churches, as well as women's, men's, and occupational affiliate groups and Bible study groups, can be powerful communities where we see many come to Christ and receive healing and deliverance. We should not fear that God will not help us. He will move in our small groups, prayer meetings, church services, and in our personal lives. He will use us as we wait and depend on His anointing and continually be filled with His Holy Spirit.

The book of Acts (which records approximately the first thirty years of the church) moves forward and the gospel of Jesus Christ rapidly spreads. Great persecution comes on the Jerusalem church, and, as a result, the believers go to other places and take the anointing with them. The church begins to impact the entire world. The disciples heal the sick, deliver those who have demons, and see multitudes come to Christ. They also become baptized and receive the infilling of the Holy Spirit.

What He Did Then He Can Do Today

In Acts 9, Paul experienced a physical manifestation of Jesus, and the Lord informed him that he was called to reach the gentiles. Paul, too, was baptized with the Holy Spirit and was powerfully used in areas of healing, the miraculous, and planting churches. He became the writer of thirteen of our New Testament books, and by the anointing of the Holy Spirit he gave eternal truths about spiritual gifts, prophecy, and Christian maturity.

Even when Paul was under house arrest, he kept his door open to anyone who wanted to experience Christ and the infilling of the Holy Spirit. The book of Acts records, "He lived there two whole years at his own expense, and welcomed all who came to him, proclaiming the kingdom of God and teaching about the Lord Jesus Christ with all boldness and without hindrance" (28:30–31 ESV).

People were powerfully used of God and the gospel of Jesus Christ rapidly moved forward. Faith—powerful faith—is greatly enhanced when we are full of the Holy Spirit. This is the key to the signs and wonders that can follow our lives. Deep inside we sense the power of God and begin to believe for the impossible. The impossible becomes possible.

Faith is the assurance of things hoped for,
the conviction of things not seen.
—Hebrews 11:1 ESV

All of us have enough faith to become saved—to be transferred from the kingdom of darkness to the kingdom of God. But many do not have a faith that is powerful, that believes in the miraculous, or that has tremendous (unusual) boldness to tell people about Jesus, pray for the sick, or deliver people from demonic activity. The infilling with the Holy Spirit is critical as we develop a powerful faith. If you have drifted or have decided that this isn't for you, take time today to think about these verses:

> On the last day of the feast, the great day, Jesus stood up and cried out, "If anyone thirsts, let him come to me and drink. Whoever believes in me, as the Scripture has said, 'Out of his heart will flow rivers of living water.'" Now this he said about the Spirit, whom those who believed in him were to receive, for as yet the Spirit had not been given, because Jesus was not yet glorified. (John 7:37–39 ESV)

> [Jesus] said to them, "These are my words that I spoke to you while I was still with you, that everything written about me in the Law of Moses and the Prophets and the Psalms must be fulfilled." Then he opened their minds to understand the Scriptures, and said to them, "Thus it is written, that the Christ should suffer and on the third day rise from the dead, and that repentance and forgiveness of sins should be proclaimed in his name to all nations, beginning from Jerusalem. You are witnesses of these things. And behold, I am sending the promise of my Father upon you. But stay in the city until you are clothed with power from on high." (Luke 24:44–49 ESV)

[Jesus] presented himself alive to them after his suffering by many proofs, appearing to them during forty days and speaking about the kingdom of God.

And while staying with them he ordered them not to depart from Jerusalem, but to wait for the promise of the Father, which, he said, "you heard from me; for John baptized with water, but you will be baptized with the Holy Spirit not many days from now."

So when they had come together, they asked him, "Lord, will you at this time restore the kingdom to Israel?" He said to them, "It is not for you to know times or seasons that the Father has fixed by his own authority. But you will receive power when the Holy Spirit has come upon you, and you will be my witnesses in Jerusalem and in all Judea and Samaria, and to the end of the earth." And when he had said these things, as they were looking on, he was lifted up, and a cloud took him out of their sight. And while they were gazing into heaven as he went, behold, two men stood by them in white robes, and said, "Men of Galilee, why do you stand looking into heaven? This Jesus, who was taken up from you into heaven, will come in the same way as you saw him go into heaven." (Acts 1:3–11 ESV)

When the day of Pentecost arrived, they were all together in one place. And suddenly there came from heaven a sound like a mighty rushing wind, and it filled the entire house where they were sitting. And divided tongues as of fire appeared to them and rested on each one of them. And they were all filled with the Holy Spirit and began to speak in other tongues as the Spirit gave them utterance. (Acts 2:1–4 ESV)

Peter, standing with the eleven, lifted up his voice and addressed them: "Men of Judea and all who dwell in

Jerusalem, let this be known to you, and give ear to my words. For these people are not drunk, as you suppose, since it is only the third hour of the day. But this is what was uttered through the prophet Joel:

'And in the last days it shall be, God declares,
that I will pour out my Spirit on all flesh,
and your sons and your daughters shall prophesy,
and your young men shall see visions,
and your old men shall dream dreams;
even on my male servants and female servants
in those days I will pour out my Spirit, and they shall prophesy.
And I will show wonders in the heavens above
and signs on the earth below,
blood, and fire, and vapor of smoke;
the sun shall be turned to darkness
and the moon to blood,
before the day of the Lord comes, the great and magnificent day. And it shall come to pass that everyone who calls upon the name of the Lord shall be saved.'"
(Acts 2:14–21 ESV)

Peter said to them, "Repent and be baptized every one of you in the name of Jesus Christ for the forgiveness of your sins, and you will receive the gift of the Holy Spirit. For the promise is for you and for your children and for all who are far off, everyone whom the Lord our God calls to himself." And with many other words he bore witness and continued to exhort them, saying, "Save yourselves from this crooked generation." So those who received his word were baptized, and there were added that day about three thousand souls.

And they devoted themselves to the apostles' teaching and the fellowship, to the breaking of bread and the prayers.

And awe came upon every soul, and many wonders and signs were being done through the apostles. And all who believed were together and had all things in common. And they were selling their possessions and belongings and distributing the proceeds to all, as any had need. And day by day, attending the temple together and breaking bread in their homes, they received their food with glad and generous hearts, praising God and having favor with all the people. And the Lord added to their number day by day those who were being saved. (Acts 2:38–47 ESV)

God Is on the Move

Do not be discouraged, for God is on the move in our world today. There are signs of revival on every continent. Although the enemy is attacking the church with viciousness, we are on the winning side. The greater the sin, the greater the grace. The more the enemy attacks us, the more supernatural power God will give us. The greater the darkness, the more the light of Jesus will shine ever more brightly. God will give you a dream, a vision, and a deep sense of anticipation about what He will do in your life.

Your faith will become supernatural. God will give you His infilling of the Holy Spirit—your courage, boldness, and belief in the supernatural will become normal. You can believe for your marriage, your family, freedom from addictions, the miraculous, visions and dreams, and you will never be the same again. Please pray with us:

Jesus, my Lord, you are the baptizer with the Holy Spirit. Baptize me now and fill me with the precious Holy Spirit. Holy Spirit, invade my life; fill me with your power and charismatic gifts. Help me to believe in your miraculous power and walk with you every moment of every day. In the wonderful name of Jesus, I pray. Amen.

17

You Can Grow in Your Faith

No human can help the helplessness of people.
We have to develop people's hearts, to believe, to think,
and to speak according to God's Word.
—Yonggi Cho

Faith is a powerful and precious spiritual reality. The presence of faith is beyond description, bringing with it tremendous joy and assurance. Once you receive this mountain-moving faith, you can overcome insurmountable obstacles in your life. It is knowledge of God's Word that lays the foundation for one to seek after God in the right way. But it is only through the power of the Holy Spirit that God imparts the needed faith into our hearts. Faith is more than understanding, it is more than hope; faith is a gift from the Lord.

It is important to remember that it usually takes time to receive increasing faith. If you do not have faith, then stop and search your heart. Confess your sins and seek after the Lord in prayer. If you want increased faith, fast and pray and read your Bible. If you do not receive more faith in a week, then continue in prayer until God imparts it to you by the power of the Holy Spirit. Be determined to grow in your faith.

When you receive the level of faith you desire, you must not let the process end there. It is just a starting point. Even when faith burns in your heart, if you do not provide a point for moving forward (stepping out), that faith will not produce results. James 2:20 says, "Faith without deeds is useless." When faith comes, something must be done or you will lose the opportunity to act. Move forward, one decision, one step, and one miracle at a time.

The Starting Point of Faith

In Mark 5:25–34, there is a story of a woman with a profound need. She wanted to be well, she wanted to live. The fact is that she had suffered for twelve years from a constant flow of blood and had visited many doctors in order to correct the problem. Long, painful treatments exhausted her finances, but she continued to grow worse. Even in her worsening condition, this woman's spirit was undefeated and her desire to live undaunted.

Very likely, she had heard about Jesus or perhaps she had watched people experience healing when He prayed for them. She was determined to connect with Jesus, her unbending spirit pleased God, and He providentially arranged circumstances for her to hear the gospel and meet Him:

> A woman was there who had been subject to bleeding for twelve years. She had suffered a great deal under the care of many doctors and had spent all she had, yet instead of getting better she grew worse. When she heard about Jesus, she came up behind him in the crowd and touched his cloak. (Mark 5:25–27)

I (Dr. Cho) am reminded of the many broken people who talk to me, sharing stories of misery, rejection, sickness, and heartache.

Many do not believe there is a way out of their circumstances; they feel it is too late. When talking with these people, I often think of the woman with the profound need. She was desperate and determined and would not give up. Finding a way to fight through the crowd, she was able to touch Jesus' garment. That determination to not give up was an act of faith. If you have a need and a desire to walk by faith, then you must be like this woman. You need to have a determination to follow through and act on your faith.

Many come for prayer, desiring to be miraculously healed, but do not take the time to read the Bible. Many do not spend time endeavoring to learn about the person of Christ. The Scripture tells us that "faith comes from hearing, and hearing through the word of Christ" (Romans 10:17 ESV). Like the diseased woman who heard of Jesus, we also must hear the words of our Lord; we need knowledge about Him and His promises. If you do not pay attention to the Word of God, which provides a solid foundation, then your faith will be greatly weakened.

The diseased woman said in her heart, *If I just touch His clothes, I will be healed*. She made touching Christ's garment the starting point of her faith. The desperation in this woman encouraged her to try to reach out:

> When she heard about Jesus, she came up behind him in the crowd and touched his cloak, because she thought, "If I just touch his clothes, I will be healed." Immediately her bleeding stopped and she felt in her body that she was freed from her suffering.
>
> At once Jesus realized that power had gone out from him. He turned around in the crowd and asked, "Who touched my clothes?" (Mark 5:27–30)

When the woman ignited her faith with action, she touched Christ's garment, the power of Christ flowed through her, and her sickness immediately left her body. Jesus felt power flow out from Him and asked, "Who touched my clothes?"

"You see the people crowding against you," his disciples answered, "and yet you can ask, 'Who touched me?'"
But Jesus kept looking around to see who had done it. Then the woman, knowing what had happened to her, came and fell at his feet, trembling, and told him the whole truth. He said to her, "Daughter, your faith has healed you. Go in peace and be freed from your suffering." (vv. 31–34)

When we are healed, see a miracle, or experience a vision or dream from God, most of us tremble. This fulfillment, which has come by faith and action, will have a great impact on us. The woman trembled and fell at Jesus' feet, telling Him of her years of sickness. Jesus recognized her faith and used this woman's story as an example of what can happen if a person takes a risk, moves ahead by faith, and believes. She was healed and blessed with the presence of Jesus.

For many Americans, every day is a day of prayer. More than half (55 percent) of Americans say they pray every day, according to a 2014 Pew Research Center survey. According to the same survey, 21 percent say they pray weekly or monthly, and 23 percent say they seldom or never pray. Even among those who are religiously unaffiliated, 20 percent say they pray daily. Women (64 percent) are more likely than men (46 percent) to pray every day. And Americans ages sixty-five and older are far more likely than adults under thirty to say they pray daily (65 percent vs. 41 percent).

The same survey also found that 45 percent of Americans—and a majority of Christians (55 percent)—say they rely a lot on prayer and personal religious reflection when making major life decisions. The same survey found that 63 percent of Christians in the US say praying regularly is an essential part of their Christian identity.[1] Many people go to church, and many people pray and perhaps understand Jesus Christ intellectually and theologically. But the head must be connected to the heart through prayer. Many know about Jesus but do not *know* Jesus. Christ's power will never be yours until you touch Him with the arm of faith.

All of us have needs. All of us go through trials and experience temptations that come from the enemy of our souls. We have all had times of discouragement, and, like this woman, we are determined to touch Jesus. No matter what anyone tells you, decide to fight on, act by faith, and fill your mind and spirit with the hundreds of Scriptures that give you the "faith" promises of God. Read those Scriptures, memorize them, and let faith grow within you. Then seek after the Lord until He imparts faith into your heart. Empower that faith into action, and begin watching the wonderful things that your heavenly Father will do in your life.

Four Decisions That Will Change Your Life

Someone has one said, "You are never too old to set another goal, or to dream a new dream."[2] As we have said, our thinking processes have tremendous attractive power. When we think right, then the right things will manifest in our lives.

Poor Thinking Patterns Must Change

The foundation for "faith thinking" is built on Jesus and the cross. When we understand the work of the cross, we can then believe and confess the promises of God for our lives. As we constantly remind ourselves of God's goodness and saturate our hearts with God's grace, we will develop habits through repetition, and faith will blossom in our thinking.

Exercising what you want in your heart makes it easier in life. For example, in marriage, we often take for granted the incredible gift of family. I (Dr. Cho) have felt that I wanted to demonstrate warmth, blessing, and to honor my wonderful wife, children, and their spouses and our grandchildren. Because I believe that I must think and say loving things, I freely tell my wife and children that I love them, and I try to be physically affectionate toward them. My positive thought is acted on and, as a result, my family better understands my deep love for them.

We have met so many Christians who have negative thoughts about themselves. It's no wonder they lack faith to believe that God is active in all their life. Some of this negative thinking comes because of their upbringing: perhaps they had parents who constantly pressured and discouraged them, friends who said negative statements about them, or have had many disappointments in life. These experiences have a tremendous effect on our lives. If this is the case with you, then remind yourself that your heavenly Father is a wonderful, merciful, kind, and gracious God who desperately loves you. You are uniquely gifted; you have abilities that no one else has. You are blessed and highly favored, and you can trust Jesus Christ in all you experience. The Holy Spirit dwells within you and will counsel and comfort you in whatever circumstances you go through.

Ask the Holy Spirit for Visions and Dreams

Once your thought pattern is on track with God, you next should ask the Holy Spirit for clear visions and dreams. Abraham was largely unknown until he received vision for his life from God. Visions and dreams are possible because they don't need money or education; we only need prayer and the help of the Holy Spirit to see dreams come to pass. The Scripture tells us, "In the last days, God says, I will pour out my Spirit on all people. Your sons and daughters will prophesy, your young men will see visions, your old men will dream dreams" (Acts 2:17). As God's beloved child, you are meant to have a vision and a dream!

Joseph had a vision when he was just seventeen years old, but all his brothers wanted to kill him along with his vision (Genesis 37). Yet he never gave up on his vision through slavery and imprisonment, but Joseph kept his vision alive until he met Pharaoh. Joseph's vision guided him to become the prime minister of Egypt.

I can vividly remember when I had my vision from God that I would have hundreds of members in a slum area of Seoul, Korea. Although I had no money, I believed in the vision and set up a tent on the street to teach the gospel to anyone who would hear. People would say to me that they pitied me because I could never build such a great church in this area. But in my heart, I saw the vision. The kingdom of God belongs to those who are "poor in spirit" (Matthew 5:3). Because I preached about Jesus Christ bringing hope to hearts, many people started coming to church.

When you read and study the Bible, you will find hope for victory in every page. You cannot receive such tremendous unfading hope from other books. The Bible alone is God's Word for your life. Even when we didn't have many church members, I would speak in a loud voice, as if I were addressing a large crowd. My mother-in-law would sometimes ask me to speak more softly. "Mother," I said, "the people I am speaking to are in the canvas of my heart. In my vision and dream, I have ten thousand people in my church. So I speak to those ten thousand people."

We should always try to visualize the result as we pray. In the Yoido Full Gospel Church, we have taught our people how to visualize success and answers to their prayers. Through visualizing and dreaming, one can incubate his or her future and thus hatch the results. God will give you revelation knowledge when you pray and listen.

Our friend Dick Eastman gives us additional insight into the power of prayer:

> Prayer gives us revelatory perception, which is necessary to triumph in the spiritual war. God promised Jeremiah, that

if he called, not only would he answer, but also, he would reveal "great and hidden things," that couldn't be understood in any other way.[3]

"Call to me and I will answer you, and will tell you great and hidden things that you have not known."
—Jeremiah 33:3 ESV

Eastman goes on to say:

The word "hidden," from the Hebrew *batsar*, is mostly translated as "isolated" or "inaccessible." It suggests that God would give Jeremiah "revelatory intuition," by revealing things that otherwise would remain isolated or inaccessible.

Such "revelatory intuition" has always been essential for the clear understanding of a victorious spiritual war. One can't pray effectively without a certain intuition about what to pray for, and also without knowing that God is truly anxious for us to seek him in prayer.[4]

As you pray, take time to listen. As you sense God's presence in your prayer closet, thoughts will form in your mind—remembering specific Scriptures might be part of how to sense the voice of God. The Holy Spirit will give you wisdom, discernment, and a sense of timing, and He will give assurance to your heart as you wait upon Him.

Have Faith and Believe

The third step is to have faith and believe. All of us have difficulties in life's circumstances with faith. I, too, have struggled with the lack of faith. I keep a mustard seed in a jar that I have frequently looked at when needing to believe for more. There have been times when I had a lot of doubt in my heart and looking at the mustard seed didn't seem to help! On one occasion, God spoke to me while I was praying and told me that just as the mustard seed is the smallest of all seeds, I only needed the smallest of faith to move mountains on His behalf.

Even if you have 99 percent doubt and only 1 percent faith, it is enough for God to move. We only need to focus on the positive, which is that we have. The fact that you are reading this book means that you have at least 1 percent of faith!

Confess with Your Mouth

Confessing with your mouth after believing with your heart is the key to seeing the hand of God move in your life. Mouth confession has tremendous power; speaking the right thing releases hope, visions and dreams, and faith. By the spoken Word of God, the world was created; likewise, your speaking will manifest that which is invisible into your life.

Language allows us to communicate with others. It is a channel for our thoughts, ideas, and feelings. Language also shapes our lives, affecting the way we think and believe. Faith and language are closely linked, which is why Paul wrote, "For it is with your heart that you believe and are justified, and it is with your mouth that you profess your faith and are saved" (Romans 10:10).

Your continuous confession of faith in God's Word is the basis for the language of faith. It is important to speak the language of faith daily. At times of great distress, speak it moment by moment. Your language of faith will change your life and affect the way you think and act.

Our hearts burn with the desire for you to speak of God's promises in your life. Refuse to listen to words of doubt and

220 • **Faith:** Believing in the God Who Works on Your Behalf

discouragement; instead, determine to stand on God's Word. If you do this, after a few days you will begin to notice more confidence, and in a few weeks you will sense a deeper assurance. When making this a daily habit (like eating or breathing), you will be amazed at what you can trust God for. Faith is believing in the God who works on your behalf. You can grow in your faith.

18

❧

Forgiving Yourself
by Faith

No child of God sins to that degree
as to make himself incapable of forgiveness.
—John Bunyan

"You aren't one of this man's disciples too, are you?"
she asked Peter.
He replied, "I am not." ...
So they asked him, "You aren't one of his disciples too, are you?"
He denied it, saying, "I am not." ...
"Didn't I see you with him in the garden?"
Again Peter denied it, and at that moment a roster began to crow.
—John 18:17, 25–27

Peter went outside and wept bitterly.
—Luke 22:62

When the right circumstances were lined up, Jesus knew Peter would deny Him. Peter didn't think it was possible. Denying Jesus was never a thought in his mind. A late-night prayer meeting in the garden of Gethsemane turned into a chaotic, dangerous moment. In the quietness of the night, soldiers came and roughly grasped Jesus. It was Peter who tried to protect Jesus and struck one of the soldiers with his sword, cutting off his ear: "And one of them struck the servant of the high priest, cutting off his right ear. But Jesus answered, 'No more of this!' And he touched the man's ear and healed him" (Luke 22:50–51; see John 18:10).

During that horrific night, the disciples didn't know how to react and it became confusing. All the disciples left and fled (Matthew 26:56). Peter decided to follow the soldiers and Jesus "at a distance" to the courtyard of the high priest. Peter was standing by, wondering what would happen. Then someone noticed him. A servant girl accused him of being with Jesus. He became frightened and said he wasn't one of His disciples, and in fact didn't even know Him. Three times Peter denied Jesus. He was overwhelmed with what he said and did, and he wept bitterly. When the situation became fearful and full of tension, Peter went AWOL. He lied and got away with it.

Much of the time, we don't think that we could say or do something that is wrong, sinful, or immoral. Ugly, harmful thoughts are not part of what we are planning on doing as we begin our day. We understand that we will experience temptation in life, but many times we are not prepared when it comes. When the circumstances are right and we are vulnerable, burned out, or emotionally tired, temptation becomes magnified. Temptation doesn't make appointments.

Peter's decision to lie, deny the Lord, and escape was driven by fear and confusion. He was shocked about what was happening to Jesus, and he became fearful for his own life. When we are frightened for ourselves, or those we love, we are often confused about what to do. It is a mental nightmare, and often we sense an urgency. At times, we feel panic, intense anxiety, and the emotional pressure to *just decide.*

We are all given the freedom to choose. Like Peter, we can choose to do the right thing or we can choose to do the wrong thing. We make our own choices to sin or to walk away from the temptation to sin. C. S. Lewis once said, "There are only two kinds of people: those who say to God, 'Thy will be done,' and those to whom God says, 'All right, then, have it your way.'"[1]

After the fact, Peter must have felt like all the air had been taken from his lungs. He likely felt sick, mentally tormented, and couldn't get the thought out of his mind, "How could I have done that?" Jesus knew that Peter would make this decision, but He also knew that He would forgive and restore Peter. In a few weeks, Peter would be full of faith once again, knowing he was forgiven, restored, and a powerful man of God. Jesus would use him to be one of the most influential apostles of all time. Our mistakes, failures, and disappointments can be our best friends—that is, if and when we learn from them.

Jesus had a plan on how He could convince Peter to know he was forgiven. Jesus had appeared to the disciples two previous times, and word was spreading among them that Jesus was resurrected from the dead. The eleven apostles talked about the future, and it didn't take long to make the decision that life had to go on. Peter and a few of the disciples decided to go fishing (John 21), which was a logical choice since they were fishermen before they followed Jesus.

They didn't catch anything all that night. In the morning, however, someone on the beach called out to them and said, "Throw your net on the other side of the boat!" They did so, and the net quickly became full with 153 fish. They couldn't believe it. They asked, "How did this happen? Who is that person who shouted to us?"

John was the first to recognize that this person was Jesus Christ. Jesus was actually there! He was on the beach, very much alive, and once again they experienced a miracle. John shouted, "It is the

Lord!" (John 21:7). Then Peter jumped in the water, and as fast as he could he went to Jesus. The others followed him in the boat. Jesus was waiting and had a fire prepared to cook breakfast for them.

Oh, how we would have liked to hear that discussion. Did Jesus speak of any details of what happened after He was crucified or give any specifics about their lives? What was the focus of the discussion? What kind of questions did the disciples ask Him? Peter must have thought about what he did, his denial of Jesus, the three denials, and how he tried to distance himself from Jesus and the disciples. Then Jesus purposely, specifically, redemptively, and lovingly focused on Peter and asked him the same question three times:

> When they had finished eating, Jesus said to Simon Peter, "Simon son of John, do you love me more than these?"
>
> "Yes, Lord," he said, "you know that I love you."
>
> Jesus said, "Feed my lambs."
>
> Again Jesus said, "Simon son of John, do you love me?"
>
> He answered, "Yes, Lord, you know that I love you."
>
> Jesus said, "Take care of my sheep."
>
> The third time he said to him, "Simon son of John, do you love me?"
>
> Peter was hurt because Jesus asked him the third time, "Do you love me?" He said, "Lord, you know all things; you know that I love you."
>
> Jesus said, "Feed my sheep." (John 21:15–17)

Forgiving Yourself

When I (Wayde) wrote the books *Why Great Men Fall*[2] and *Success Kills*,[3] I frequently thought of the many people who have made mistakes, failed, or were deeply wounded by a decision they had made. I've talked with and counseled hundreds of leaders, friends, and acquaintances who have made similar decisions as Peter. I, too, have made mistakes, bad judgment calls, and have been wrong—many times. In fact, all of us have.

The pain, rejection, and disappointment we have with ourselves can cause us to withdraw, hide from others, and avoid responsibilities. These experiences can be a tremendous "faith drain" that will sap our strength and take our hope of being successful again. When we have this kind of disposition, the enemy of our souls will attack us in any way he possibly can. We are weak and he will endeavor to totally break us down and destroy any hopes and dreams we had. Over thousands of years of history, the enemy has repeatedly attacked those who are weak because of their discouragement.

Satan never offers hope, nor will he encourage us to try again; he only offers condemnation and haunting thoughts of hopelessness. When Peter denied the Lord three times, he wept bitterly. He couldn't believe that he was so weak. The agony that he must have felt was beyond description. He failed, lied, denied Christ, and pretended he did not know Him. In his heart, Peter felt the emptiness of rejecting the one he had given his life to, the one who had loved him more deeply than anyone else could. Because of fear, Peter made the decision to do the wrong thing. C. S. Lewis] said, "God allows us to experience the low points of life in order to teach us lessons that we could learn in no other way."[4]

If you have sinned, made bad decisions, or done something of which you feel you can never be forgiven, you might feel you will never be the same because of what you have done. Discouragement, guilt, and shame are emotions that will sap your strength, and you may feel that having faith to forgive yourself is next to impossible.

People can live a lifetime of feeling shame and guilt. You do not need to live this way. In fact, your bad decisions, mistakes, and failures can be your friends. You can experience *total* forgiveness and learn from your mistakes. All of us have made wrong decisions, and all of us are sinners (Romans 3:10, 23; 1 John 1:8), but we can use these decisions to become wiser.

Moving On and Walking by Faith

You can have faith that God forgives you of every sin, bad decision, and mistake you have made. In fact, He not only forgives you but will also use your experiences for your good (Romans 8:28)—yes, even your failures, sins, and bad decisions.

You might feel like a bad person or that you're living a lie. Perhaps you have hurt your family members, people you go to church with, or your friends. If you are a leader of an organization or a church, your feelings of embarrassment and shame of what you did are always present in your mind, pressuring you to think that God hasn't forgiven you or that you will never be restored. A constant companion likely is this thought: *I'll never be the same because of what I did.*

If you have sincerely committed your life to Jesus Christ and made Him Lord of your life (see Romans 10:9–10; 1 John 2:1), then He has completely forgiven you of everything you have ever done. You have total forgiveness in Christ Jesus. You have been adopted into His family and are a child of God (John 1:12). This is a fact, and nothing you think or anything others might tell you can change that. The Scripture says, "Therefore, there is now no condemnation for those who are in Christ Jesus" (Romans 8:1).

Don't trust your emotions or feelings; they are fickle and undependable and will only lead you to think that complete forgiveness and future success are impossible. Feelings of shame, overwhelming guilt, and discouragement are common emotions that we all feel when we fail.

You might feel that you are forever handicapped because of your past behavior. By faith, you can believe what He has done for you by His death on the cross and His physical resurrection from the dead. Study the promises in the Bible and believe that those promises are for you. God does not lie or play games; He has promised that He has forgiven you, which means you are justified and redeemed by His precious blood. You only need to have faith in what He did for you.

When you are struggling with thoughts that you are not forgiven, or satan is telling you that you cannot ever be forgiven, then you need to pray by faith. Talk to your heavenly Father and ask Him to help you forgive yourself. The memory of what you did in the past condemns you, but Jesus Christ doesn't condemn you. You might be disgusted with yourself, full of guilt and shame, but Jesus looks at you with absolute love. The truth is that He gave His life for every sin that you have committed—past, present and future. John writes:

> This is how we know that we belong to the truth and how we set our hearts at rest in his presence: If our hearts condemn us, we know that God is greater than our hearts, and he knows everything. (1 John 3:19–20)

If God has forgiven you, then shouldn't you also forgive yourself? Begin to praise and thank God that He has forgiven you. Do this repeatedly, remembering that your words have tremendous power. Forgiveness is a fact, and you must tell yourself that you have been forgiven and that God has a wonderful future for you.

Ask God to heal your memories and free you from your past. Past decisions can paralyze you, causing you to freeze, and inhibiting you as you try to move forward. If possible, go to those people you have hurt—go to your family, friends, leaders, employees, and anyone you feel that you have offended, asking God to help you in His timing to communicate to them and let them know that you regret what you have done and are sorry. You can ask for forgiveness and tell them you hope that they can forgive, even as Christ has forgiven you.

Total Forgiveness

Many call 1 Corinthians 13 the great love chapter of the Bible. In this definition of love, we are told that *agape* love "keeps no record of wrongs" (v. 5). This is a perfect expression and example of the result of total forgiveness. *Logizoma* is the Greek word that is translated as "no record." This means not to calculate or credit—there is no record. "Love [*agape*] does not dishonor others, it is not self-seeking, it is not easily angered, it keeps *no record* of wrongs" (1 Corinthians 13:5). Furthermore, Romans 4:5 explains, "However, to the one who does not work but trusts God who justifies the ungodly, their faith is *credited as righteousness*". The same word is also used in 1 Corinthians 13:5. If you believe that your faith is "credited as righteousness," then you can have assurance that there is "no record" of your sins.

Forgiving yourself means that you experience the love that keeps no evidence of your wrongs. For many, this is a difficult truth to assimilate. People can continue to permit their thoughts to be condemning, or listen to others who remind him them of their past behavior or sinful activity, but the evidence is not there. There is no record of our wrongs!

I (Wayde) have often have heard, "I can forgive others, but how can I ever forget what I have done? I know God forgives me, but I can't forgive myself." Forgiving ourselves is something we do all our lives. Here are some reasons why we can't forgive ourselves.

Anger and disappointment toward ourselves can overpower our emotions. It is common to be angry, greatly ashamed, and disappointed with oneself. We look back to what we said and did, and the price we paid for our behavior. Some people become so angry with themselves that they even have thoughts of harming themselves.

Look at the Old Testament story of Joseph: "Then Joseph said to his brothers... 'And now, do not be distressed and do not be angry with yourselves for selling me here, because it was to save lives that

God sent me ahead of you'" (Genesis 45:4–5). His brothers were frightened that Joseph would hold a grudge and so were angry with themselves for what they did. They probably worried about him for years, and they lived with their lie.

Joseph was not going to harm them, and, as a matter of fact, he would go on to greatly bless them. He didn't want them to be angry with themselves, and he didn't want them to avoid him. That is the way God forgives each and every one of us. Jesus does not want us to be angry with ourselves for our sins, and He certainly doesn't want us to hide from Him either.

Not forgiving ourselves fosters feelings of tremendous insecurity and can keep us from reaching our potential in Christ. We think or say negative, defeating words that bring further harm to our view of ourselves. Joseph's brothers could not take back what they had done; they hated their decision of selling Joseph into slavery. God will take the wasted years of your life and restore them. You will make wiser decisions, grow in character, and have a greater ability to understand others and walk by faith. God promises, "I will repay you for the years the locusts have eaten" (Joel 2:25).

In some cases, it is fear more than anger that is a barrier to us forgiving ourselves. This fear can come from hurt, rejection, trauma, or bad experiences. Much of the time our fears can come from what we have done. We regret our behavior, which leads to guilt, and guilt can lead to fear. We think of "what might have been." And so we fear that what we did, or what was done to us, cannot possibly turn out for good, thus creating a guilt that we live with.

True Guilt and False Guilt

There are two kinds of guilt that most of us struggle with: true guilt (a result of our sin against God) and false guilt (when there is no sin in our lives). When we have sinned, the Bible is clear that we must confess it to God (1 John 1:9; 2:1). The blood of Jesus takes care of true guilt by doing two basic things: it washes away our sin—as though it never had existed—and it perfectly satisfies God's eternal justice. Sin that has been confessed to God is totally forgiven by Him. Any guilt we feel after that is false guilt, which has nothing to do with what's true and accurate. Nor is it related to true repentance. Rather, it is usually the fear of disapproval in disguise.

False guilt consumes our thinking while we are awake and asleep, creating in our lives both spiritual and psychological cataracts, stopping us from seeing our relationships with God, others, and ourselves clearly. Through false guilt, we lie to and bear false witness against ourselves.[5] The three kinds of false guilt come when *sin has been forgiven* by God, when sin *was never involved* in the first place, and when we care *too much* for people in great need (vicarious trauma and compassion fatigue).

False Guilt: Sin Has Been Forgiven by God

False guilt comes when we have confessed our sins but we do not *feel* forgiven. Once we have acknowledged our sin, we accept our forgiveness and leave the rest in God's hands by faith. By not forgiving ourselves, this is a subtle way of competing with Christ's atonement. Jesus died for our sins, bore our transgressions, and paid the price for our sins (2 Corinthians 5:17). Instead of accepting Jesus' sacrifice, however, many want to punish themselves for their failures. This type of behavior does nothing more than resists God's wonderful grace and total forgiveness. Paul wrote:

> When you were dead in your sins and in the uncircumcision of your flesh, God made you alive with Christ. *He forgave us all our sins*, having canceled the charge of our legal indebtedness, which stood against us and condemned us; he has taken it away, nailing it to the cross. (Colossians 2:13–14)

Many do not forgive themselves because of the fear of not being forgiven, or they tell themselves, *Now I will never reach my full potential.* The person who fears has not been made perfect in love, and fear "has to do with punishment" (1 John 4:18). We need to understand that fear—and punishing ourselves for our mistakes—is not pleasing to God. This will only bring us discouragement, sadness, and oftentimes make us hard to live with. It is unhealthy and we need to make the decision to walk away from our past failures and sins and *not look back.* Move on; forgive yourself and anyone who has hurt you.

False Guilt: When Sin Isn't Involved

The emotion of false guilt can be very real at times, even when sin isn't involved. Even though there is no evidence for the sense of guilt, we still feel it anyway. An example of this would be a mom who is lovingly caring for her small child and the child accidently hurts himself. Repeatedly, the mom says to herself, *If only I had been next to my child when this happened,* or *If only we would have been in the other room.* "If only, if only, if only!" These kinds of feelings can be overwhelming, but there was no intentional mistake. There was no sin. But the guilt is still real.

False Guilt: Compassion Fatigue

Vicarious trauma (or compassion fatigue) can also be a reason that we feel guilty. I (Wayde) have met many caring people, leaders, and pastors who are overwhelmed because they could not do enough to help others. They work day and night to help people, and thus experience their own trauma. This is another kind of false guilt.

When we care so much for people but can't do everything that needs to be done, we feel guilty. Those who care have been greatly involved in people's traumatic experiences (loss, death, divorce, abuse, poverty, natural disaster, or war) and are often full of shock and trauma themselves. It is a frequent emotion when we are involved in helping people who have had tragic experiences.

When helping people in need, the emotions the people have can have a deep impact on us. We can feel guilt, experience shock, and have feelings of trauma too. With this kind of false guilt, we need to remind ourselves that *we can't do everything* that needs to be done. We can only do our best and trust God with the rest. This kind of false guilt is often called "the cost of caring." But not only is there false guilt—there is true guilt that we can experience as well.

True Guilt and Grace

The initial work of the Holy Spirit is that He convicts us of sin. When we walk in the light, we know His blood cleanses us of sin, but walking in the light also reveals sin in us that we may not have seen before (1 John 1:7–8). We are temples of the Holy Spirit, and He is our Counselor, Advocate, and Helper. He will frequently speak to us about what to do and what we have done. When we decide to do or say something that is not pleasing to God, the Holy Spirit will speak to us and we will feel a sense of guilt.

The sense of guilt God instigates is only temporary; He only uses it to get our attention. When we say, "I'm sorry" or "Forgive me," and are sincere about it, God completely forgives us. And so the ability to forgive ourselves encompasses our understanding of grace, which is undeserved favor. Mercy is not getting what we deserve (justice), while grace is accepting what we don't deserve (complete forgiveness). We have been reconciled to God by what Jesus Christ did for us on the cross.[6]

Some feel that forgiveness may seem unfair when we have done something wrong. We keep telling ourselves that we have let God down, we have let others down, people were hurt, and so how could our behavior ever be forgiven? Many want to punish themselves because of their sin. But will you not accept what Jesus did for you? The blood of Jesus covers all your sins. The price that Jesus paid is beyond description. God does not desire anything else; Jesus paid the total price.

All accusations regarding confessed sin come from the devil, which works either as a roaring lion to scare us or as an angel of light to deceive us (1 Peter 5:8; 2 Corinthians 11:14). The enemy will push, accuse, cause us to fear, and endeavor to do anything he can to convince us that we are not forgiven. But we must abide in Jesus, depend on the Holy Spirit, and remind ourselves that perfect love drives out fear (1 John 4:18).

The bottom line is this: not forgiving ourselves is wrong and we have made the decision to not believe God's Word. In doing that, we are not taking God at His word and we are not accepting what Jesus did for us on the cross. Permit God to use the shame, guilt, and sorrow that you feel about what you have done to draw you to Him and not push you away from Him. He will not give up on you. He will continually endeavor to show you His love and forgiveness.

Let Go of the Past

The wonderful grace of God in your life is that when you have been forgiven, He keeps no record of wrongs. When you comprehend this truth, you let go of the past and you walk by faith into your future. God will use *all things* for your good, even your failures, mistakes, and sins, which is why God spoke to Jeremiah, saying, "If you repent, I will restore you that you may serve me; if you utter worthy, not worthless, words, you will be my spokesman" (Jeremiah 15:19).

We cast our care on God and rely on Him to restore us and to cause everything to turn out for good. Our lives might be different; however, God will use all our experiences for our good when we depend on Him. God promises us, "For I know the plans I have for you … plans to prosper you and not to harm you, plans to give you hope and a future" (Jeremiah 29:11).

When we forgive ourselves by faith, we accept ourselves and discontinue condemning ourselves. We forgive ourselves just as God forgives. We have memories of past behaviors, but we are free of guilt and full of thankfulness. We all have a sin nature and are flawed in our humanness. God completely knows us and understands that we have potential to sin. If and when this happens, we must again go to God for His forgiveness and grace.

Adam and Eve, Moses, Abraham, David, Jonah, and Peter (and many others)—all these people had to forgive themselves before they could move into the future that God had planned for them. The Bible is full of people who have made bad decisions, failed, and sinned but have been forgiven. It's time for you to move on and walk by faith in your righteousness.

If we believe in the love of God, we can conquer guilt and shame. We can change, develop, and grow. We can forgive others and ourselves. We become better people, more spiritually alert and developing a depth of understanding God's marvelous grace. By faith you can believe that your mistakes, failures, and sins will be forgiven and forgotten. With God's grace, we can conquer anything. God has worked and is working on your behalf. C. S. Lewis said, "I think that if God forgives us we must forgive ourselves. Otherwise, it is almost like setting up ourselves as a higher tribunal than Him."[7]

Faith, Hope, and Love

Paul concluded the love chapter by writing, "And now these three remain: faith, hope and love. But the greatest of these is love" (1 Corinthians 13:13). When discussing the many topics of this book, Pastor Cho and I (Wayde) frequently spoke about faith, hope, and love. I asked him what he believed was the greatest need in the body of Christ today.

Pastor Cho said, "People need hope. Faith itself is hope and has the power to make all things new." He continued, "We live in a time of tremendous attack from the enemy. He is attacking the hope that Christ gives to us." For some time, we discussed this topic and concluded that if we could encourage Christians to have dynamic faith in the truths found in the Bible, then they would have wonderful hope and in turn would love people beyond their human ability—with God's *agape* love.

As followers of Jesus Christ, we must believe that everything is possible through faith. Even if you have the faith of a mustard seed, you can believe for the impossible. It is our prayer that through the words and biblical principles that are given in this book that you will grow in your faith in Jesus Christ and in all that He has promised you. Through the numerous examples of the miraculous story of the Yoido Full Gospel Church and Dr. Cho's personal life, we pray that you will be greatly encouraged to believe.

Faith Scriptures for Meditation

Living by faith does not come naturally. To live by faith, we need the help of the Holy Spirit. As believers, we are temples of the Holy Spirit and He will help us grow in our faith and walk by faith. But we must pray, and, as a result, we will have dreams and visions. Our faith is demonstrated by speaking words that encourage and strengthen faith. When we make every effort to do this, our heavenly Father is pleased and will move through our faith.

Even though our eyes cannot see through a problem, nor our ears hear words of encouragement, nor our hands feel results in the face of suffering, we must nevertheless stand firm on the Word of God and speak, "I am in Christ, so 'I can do all things' with His help (Philippians 4:13). I can do this. Lord, help me do it." We confess words of encouragement, success, good health, and spiritual strength. We permit our minds to be transformed by the truths found in Scripture. When we speak to ourselves the words of truth, that word will connect with our spirit, soul, and body.

God is the God who quickens the dead and calls things that are not as though they are (Romans 4:17). We are His children, and although we might feel doubt, we can be determined to not waver because of changing circumstances but stand firm on the Word of God. We can speak creatively and experience the Father's miracles in our lives. Our confession of the truths of the Word of God build our faith. When our thinking is confused, or we are obsessed with the constant bad news we hear from the media or in conversations, we can quote God's Word and think clearly.

The Power of Words

But what does it say? "The word is near you; it is in your mouth and in your heart," that is, the message concerning faith that we proclaim: If you declare with your mouth, "Jesus is Lord," and believe in your heart that God raised him from the dead, you will be saved. For it is with your heart that you believe and are justified, and it is with your mouth that you profess your faith and are saved. (Romans 10:8–10)

Encouraging Words Help When We Are Anxious

Anxiety weighs down the heart,
    but a kind word cheers it up. (Proverbs 12:25)

Wise Words Bring Healing

The words of the reckless pierce like swords,
    but the tongue of the wise brings healing.
    (Proverbs 12:18)

Dear friend, I pray that you may enjoy good health and that all may go well with you, even as your soul is getting along well. (3 John 2)

Carefully Chosen Words Help Keep Us from Trouble

Those who guard their mouths and their tongues
    keep themselves from calamity. (Proverbs 21:23)

Controlling What We Say Protects Us

Keep your tongue from evil
and your lips from telling lies. (Psalm 34:13)

Deciding Not to Sin with Our Words Protects Us

I said, "I will watch my ways
and keep my tongue from sin;
I will put a muzzle on my mouth
while in the presence of the wicked." (Psalm 39:1)

Praying We Use the Right Words Brings Honor to God

May these words of my mouth
and this meditation of my heart
be pleasing in your sight,
LORD, my Rock and my Redeemer. (Psalm 19:14)

Believing by Faith

Faith Is Credited to Us as Righteousness

Abram believed the LORD, and he credited it to him as righteousness. (Genesis 15:6)

Faith Pleases God

Without faith it is impossible to please him, for whoever would draw near to God must believe that he exists and that he rewards those who seek him. (Hebrews 11:6)

Faith Helps Us Do What Jesus Did

"And these signs will accompany those who believe: In my name they will drive out demons; they will speak in new tongues; they will pick up snakes with their hands; and when they drink deadly poison, it will not hurt them at all; they will place their hands on sick people, and they will get well." (Mark 16:17–18)

Faith Overcomes Fear

"Do not fear, for I am with you;
    do not be dismayed, for I am your God.
I will strengthen you and help you;
    I will uphold you with my righteous right hand."
    (Isaiah 41:10)

Faith Helps Us Overcome Worry and Anxiety

Cast all your anxiety on him because he cares for you. (1 Peter 5:7)

Do not be anxious about anything, but in every situation, by prayer and petition, with thanksgiving, present your requests to God. And the peace of God, which transcends all understanding, will guard your hearts and your minds in Christ Jesus. (Philippians 4:6–7)

Faith Believes God's Peace Is Promised

"Peace I leave with you; my peace I give you. I do not give to you as the world gives. Do not let your hearts be troubled and do not be afraid." (John 14:27)

Faith Brings Victory over Despair and Broken Experiences

I waited patiently for the LORD;
    he turned to me and heard my cry.
He lifted me out of the slimy pit,
    out of the mud and mire;
he set my feet on a rock
    and gave me a firm place to stand.

He put a new song in my mouth,
  a hymn of praise to our God.
Many will see and fear the LORD
  and put their trust in him. (Psalm 40:1–3)

The righteous cry out, and the LORD hears them;
  he delivers them from all their troubles. (Psalm 34:17)

But those who hope in the LORD
  will renew their strength.
They will soar on wings like eagles;
  they will run and not grow weary,
  they will walk and not be faint. (Isaiah 40:31)

Faith Gives Assurance That There Is a Wonderful Place in Heaven Prepared

"Do not let your hearts be troubled. You believe in God; believe also in me. My Father's house has many rooms; if that were not so, would I have told you that I am going there to prepare a place for you? And if I go and prepare a place for you, I will come back and take you to be with me that you also may be where I am." (John 14:1–3)

Faith Gives Courage When We Feel Insecure, Weak, or Fearful

"Be strong and courageous. Do not be afraid or terrified because of them, for the LORD your God goes with you; he will never leave you nor forsake you." (Deuteronomy 31:6)

Surely the righteous will never be shaken;
  they will be remembered forever.
They will have no fear of bad news;
  their hearts are steadfast, trusting in the LORD.
Their hearts are secure, they will have no fear;

in the end they will look in triumph on their foes.
(Psalm 112:6–8)

You are my hiding place;
   you will protect me from trouble
      and surround me with songs of deliverance.
   I will instruct you and teach you in the way you should go;
   I will counsel you with my loving eye on you.
   (Psalm 32:7–8)

Faith Encourages Us to Not Give Up

So do not throw away your confidence; it will be richly rewarded. You need to persevere so that when you have done the will of God, you will receive what he has promised. For, "In just a little while, he who is coming will come and will not delay." And, "But my righteous one will live by faith. And I take no pleasure in the one who shrinks back." But we do not belong to those who shrink back and are destroyed, but to those who have faith and are saved. (Hebrews 10:35–39)

You will keep in perfect peace
   those whose minds are steadfast,
      because they trust in you.
   Trust in the LORD forever,
   for the LORD, the LORD himself, is the Rock eternal
   (Isaiah 26:3–4)

Faith Helps Us Understand the Value of Waiting for God's Timing

Be patient, then, brothers and sisters, until the Lord's coming. See how the farmer waits for the land to yield its valuable crop, patiently waiting for the autumn and spring rains. You too, be patient and stand firm, because the Lord's coming is near. (James 5:7–8)

Be still before the LORD
 and wait patiently for him;
do not fret when people succeed in their ways,
 when they carry out their wicked schemes. (Psalm 37:7)

Faith Helps Us Know God Is with Us

What, then, shall we say in response to these things? If God is for us, who can be against us? He who did not spare his own Son, but gave him up for us all—how will he not also, along with him, graciously give us all things? (Romans 8:31–32)

"For I am the LORD your God
 who takes hold of your right hand
and says to you, Do not fear;
 I will help you.
Do not be afraid, you worm Jacob,
 little Israel, do not fear,
for I myself will help you," declares the LORD,
 your Redeemer, the Holy One of Israel. (Isaiah 41:13–14)

Keep your lives free from the love of money and be content with what you have, because God has said,
 "Never will I leave you;
 never will I forsake you."
So we say with confidence,
 "The Lord is my helper; I will not be afraid.
  What can mere mortals do to me?"

Remember your leaders, who spoke the word of God to you. Consider the outcome of their way of life and imitate their faith. (Hebrews 13:5–7)

In peace I will lie down and sleep,
> for you alone, Lord,
> make me dwell in safety. (Psalm 4:8)

"Though the mountains be shaken
> and the hills be removed,
yet my unfailing love for you will not be shaken
> nor my covenant of peace be removed,"
> says the Lord, who has compassion on you. (Isaiah 54:10)

"I will not leave you as orphans; I will come to you."
(John 14:18)

In all your ways submit to him,
> and he will make your paths straight. (Proverbs 3:6)

I am not saying this because I am in need, for I have learned
to be content whatever the circumstances. I know what it is
to be in need, and I know what it is to have plenty. I have
learned the secret of being content in any and every situation, whether well fed or hungry, whether living in plenty
or in want. I can do all this through him who gives me
strength. (Philippians 4:11–13)

Faith Trusts God When Others Bring Harm or Intimidation

Refrain from anger and turn from wrath;
> do not fret—it leads only to evil.
For those who are evil will be destroyed,
> but those who hope in the Lord will inherit the land.
A little while, and the wicked will be no more;
> though you look for them, they will not be found.
(Psalm 37:8–10)

"You will not have to fight this battle. Take up your positions; stand firm and see the deliverance the Lord will give you, Judah and Jerusalem. Do not be afraid; do not be discouraged. Go out to face them tomorrow, and the Lord will be with you." (2 Chronicles 20:17)

Faith Trusts God in All Circumstances

For in this hope we were saved. But hope that is seen is no hope at all. Who hopes for what they already have? But if we hope for what we do not yet have, we wait for it patiently.

In the same way, the Spirit helps us in our weakness. We do not know what we ought to pray for, but the Spirit himself intercedes for us through wordless groans. (Romans 8:24–26)

And we know that in all things God works for the good of those who love him, who have been called according to his purpose. (Romans 8:28)

Consider it pure joy, my brothers and sisters, whenever you face trials of many kinds, because you know that the testing of your faith produces perseverance. Let perseverance finish its work so that you may be mature and complete, not lacking anything. (James 1:2–4)

I will stand at my watch
    and station myself on the ramparts;
I will look to see what he will say to me,
    and what answer I am to give to this complaint.
Then the Lord replied:
    "Write down the revelation
        and make it plain on tablets
        so that a herald may run with it.
For the revelation awaits an appointed time;

it speaks of the end
and will not prove false.
Though it linger, wait for it;
it will certainly come
and will not delay." (Habakkuk 2:1–3)

"I tell you, he will see that they get justice, and quickly. However, when the Son of Man comes, will he find faith on the earth?" (Luke 18:8)

Acknowledgments

To Rosalyn (Wayde's wife) for always being there to edit, change, listen and assist us in writing. (She has been a full-time college professor in English, research, business, and all types of writing.) What a gifted person!

To the incredible leaders at BroadStreet Publishing: Carlton Garborg (president), David Sluka (editorial director), Bill Watkins (senior editor), Michelle Winger (administrative director), Ryan Adair (primary editor on this book), and other leaders such as Bill Schultz, Amy Schultz, Sam Klejwa, Natalie Ruffing, Suzanne Niles, Kendall Moon, and their support staff. From the president through all of the BroadStreet support staff, they have been extraordinarily helpful, patient, and gracious.

To Dr. Yong Hoon Lee, senior pastor of the Yoido Full Gospel Church, who is an incredible leader and pastor with wonderful skills and unusual sensitivities to the Holy Spirit. I (Dr. Cho) will always be grateful for Dr. Lee's friendship, loyalty, kindness to me, and his tender care for our church.

To Reverend Jeffrey Yoon, director of Church Growth International—his advice, helpful information, and assisting with dates and events have been invaluable.

We want to give our heartfelt thanks to the Assemblies of God missionaries who have deeply impacted our lives. Over the years they have provided godly and dedicated missionaries to the work in Korea. From my (Dr. Cho) early days as a Christian until now, they have sacrificially given their ministry gifts to me and the people of Korea.

We are grateful to the Assemblies of God for assisting us with information, archives, and advice in the writing of this book. The World Missions department has been such a gift to the work in Korea.

Endnotes

1. Born Again: How My Walk of Faith Began

1 Wayde and Rosalyn Goodall, *The Blessing: Experiencing the Power of the Holy Spirit* (Lake Mary, FL: Creation House, 2005), 87–90.

2. Faith and Dreams

1 Wayde and Rosalyn Goodall, *Principles of Counseling* (Springfield, MO: Africa's Hope), n.p. Dr. Wayde and Rosalyn discuss biblical counseling principles that assist pastors, lay leaders, and counselors as they help people through counseling.

2 "Mother Teresa Quotes," Catholic Answers Forums, http://forums.catholic.com/showthread.php?t=979550, September 23, 2015.

3 "Thoreau Quotes," The Thoreau Society, http://www.chebucto.ns.ca/Philosophy/Sui-Generis/Thoreau/quotes.htm.

4 "Mary Kay Quotes," Inspirational Words of Wisdom, http://www.wow4u.com/mary-kay-ash2/index.html.

5 *Webster's Third New International Dictionary*, unabridged, s.v. "wish," http://unabridged.merriam-webster.com.

6 Groopman, *The Anatomy of Hope: How People Prevail in the Face of Illness* (New York: Random House, 2004), xvi.

7 A denarius is about a day's wage for a laborer.

3. Being Led by the Spirit

1 ITI, eds., *Pastor's Prayer Life in the Holy Spirit and Prayer: A Spiritual Program for the Pastors* (Seoul, Korea: Templeprayer.com).

2 Adapted from Dr. David Yonggi Cho, *The Fourth Dimension: Discovering a New World of Answered Prayer* (Newberry, FL: Bridge-Logos Publishers, 1989), 113–120.

3 Adapted from Cho, *The Fourth Dimension*, 88.

4. The Principles of Faith

1 "Yonggi has always liked to read any books he could get, and he would read them all the way through. Our father didn't want him to read the Bible because of his health. Yonggi would read under the covers in the dark with a light bulb. He wanted to read and understand English, so he practiced memorizing the English dictionary. He practiced writing English words on the bottom of a water bowl—he wrote the words seven times until he had memorized the words. Because of his knowledge of English (his doctors didn't know he understood English), when his doctors talked (in English) saying, 'This boy will not live very long,' he understood them. Even though he was dying, he had a big dream." (This was related in a conversation with Cho Hae Sook, Yonggi Cho's eldest sister, and Wayde and Rosalyn Goodall.)

5. What Weakens Our Faith

1 David Yonggi Cho, *How Can I Be Healed?* (Seoul, Korea: Logos Co., International Theological Institute), "Foreword."

6. Listening to the Holy Spirit

1 Adapted from *Church Growth Manual No. 7* (Yoido, Korea: Church Growth International).

2 Excerpted by permission from Jack Hayford, *Spirit Filled: The Overflowing Power of the Holy Spirit* (Los Angeles: Jack Hayford Ministries, 1984, 2007), n.p.

7. What Is Faith?

1 David Yonggi Cho, "Living by Faith, Not by Sight" (Seoul, Korea: David Cho Evangelistic Mission, Spring 2006), 3.

2 Henry David Thoreau Quotes, BrainyQuote, https://www.brainyquote.com/quotes/quotes/h/henrydavid141463.html.

3 "Billy Graham's Einstein Speech," Inspire21, www.Inspire21.com/stories/faith stories/BillyGrahamsEinsteinSpeech.

9. Confidence That Builds Faith

1 Warren W. Wiersbe, *The Bible Exposition Commentary* (Colorado Springs, CO: Chariot Victor Publishing), vol. 2, 317.

2 Ibid., 317–18.

10. The Demonstration of Faith

1 J. Oswald Sanders, AZ Quotes, http://www.azquotes.com/quote/662517.

2 *Webster's Third New International Dictionary*, unabridged, s.v. "reward," http://unabridged.merriam-webster.com.

11. Heroes of Faith: Things Are Not as They Seem

1 John W. Kennedy, "Pastor Jack Hayford: Christians should not expect to escape the coming persecution," Charisma News, August 18, 2015, http://www.charismanews.com/world/51086-pastor-jack-hayford-christians-should-not-expect-to-escape-the-coming-persecution.

Section III Walking by Faith

1 Billy Graham, "Answers," January 1, 2015, Billygraham.org.

12. Faithfulness: The Foundation of Faith

1 This chapter was adapted from Wayde Goodall and Thomas Trask, *The Fruit of the Spirit: Becoming the Person God Wants You to Be* (Grand Rapids, MI: Zondervan, 2000). Used by permission.

2 Phillip Yancy, *The Jesus I Never Knew* (Grand Rapids: Zondervan, 1995), 258–259.

3 David Jeremiah, *God in You* (Sisters, OR: Multnomah, 1998), 83.

4 Max Lucado, *When God Whispers Your Name* (Dallas, TX: Word, 1994), 32–33.

5 "The Pioneer Missions," NASA, March 26, 2007, https://www.nasa.gov/centers/ames/missions/archive/pioneer.html.

6 Honor Books Staff, eds., *God's Treasury of Virtues* (Tulsa, OK: Honor Books, 1996), 323.

7 Ray Steadman, *The Nature of Prayer* and *Jesus Teaches on Prayer*, www.RayStedman.com.

13. Hope

1 Groopman, *The Anatomy of Hope*, xiv.

2 Jürgen Moltmann, *Theology of Hope* (Minneapolis, MN: Fortress Press, 1993), 21.

3 Groopman, *The Anatomy of Hope*, 81.

4 William Barclay, *New Testament Words* (Louisville, KY: John Knox Press, 1974), 76.

5 Jürgen Moltmann, *The Source of Life: The Holy Spirit and the Theology of Life* (Minneapolis, MN: Fortress Press, 1997), 40.

14. Prayer: The Cry of Faith

1 *Matthew Henry's Concise Commentary*, http://biblehub.com/commentaries/exodus/15-25.htm.

2 Bill Gothard, *The Power of Crying Out: When Prayer Becomes Mighty* (Colorado Springs, CO: Multnomah Books, 2012), 12.

3 Bob Paulson, "Crying Out to God for a Darkening Nation," March 19, 2016, Billy Graham Evangelistic Association, www.billygraham.org/decision-magazine/april-2016/crying-out-to-god-for-a-darkening-nation/.

4 Ibid.

5 BGEA Staff, "Answers," June 1, 2004, Billy Graham Evangelistic Association, https://billygraham.org/answer/what-is-prayer/.

15. Be Confident in Your Faith

1 Francis McNutt, *The Nearly Perfect Crime: How the Church Almost Killed the Ministry of Healing* (Grand Rapids, MI: Chosen Books, 2005), 162–163.

2 C. S. Lewis, http://www.cslewisinstitute.org/Christianity_Makes_Sense_of_the_World. This famous quote by C. S. Lewis comes from a paper given to The Oxford Socratic Club entitled "Is Theology Poetry?" Lewis sets out to answer the question, is the imagination of followers of Jesus so aroused and satisfied by the poetry of the gospel message that they have mistaken intellectual assent for mere aesthetic enjoyment? In other words, has the romantic attraction of the story of Jesus trumped the place of reason in coming to faith?

16. Faith, Power, and Impartation

1 Acts 1:3 states that Jesus spent forty days with the apostles, presenting "himself alive after his suffering by many proofs." Ten days after the ascension was the day of Pentecost, which was when the disciples were baptized with the Holy Spirit.

17. You Can Grow in Your Faith

1 Michael Lipka, "5 facts about Prayer," May 4, 2016, Pew Research Center, http://www.pewresearch.org/fact-tank/2016/05/04/5-facts-about-prayer/.

2 This often-quoted statement is frequently cited as a statement from C. S. Lewis, but it is a disputed quote, which is why we cited it as anonymous.

3 Dick Eastman, "Going Further in the Spiritual War (War of the Faith)," http://www.angelfire.com/sc3/wedigmontana/War.html.

4 Ibid.

18. Forgiving Yourself by Faith

1 Quoted in Wayne A. Detzler, *New Testament Words in Today's Language* (Colorado Springs, CO: Victor Books, 1986), 185.

2 Wayde Goodall, *Why Great Men Fall: 15 Winning Strategies to Rise Above It All* (Green Forest, AR: New Leaf Press, 2005).

3 Wayde Goodall, *Success Kills: Sidestepping the Snares That Will Steal Your Dream* (Green Forest, AR: New Leaf Press, 2009).

4 C. S. Lewis, "Quotable Quote," Goodreads, http://www.goodreads.com/quotes/128982-god-allows-us-to-experience-the-low-points-of-life.

5 Paul Coughlin, "Healthy Guilt vs. False and Harmful Guilt," Living without Constant Guilt series, Focus on the Family, http://www.focusonthefamily.com/lifechallenges/emotional-health/living-without-constant-guilt/living-without-constant-guilt-how-to-avoid-relational-destruction-with-god-others-and-ourselves.

6 Christian Answers Network experts, "Atonement," *Bible Encyclopedia*, http://www.christiananswers.net/dictionary/atonement.html. "The meaning of the word is simply at-one-ment, i.e., the state of being at one or being reconciled, so atonement is reconciliation. Thus, it is used to denote the effect which flows from the death of Christ."

7 W. H. Lewis, *Letters of C. S. Lewis* (Orlando, FL: Houghton Mifflin Harcourt, 1966), 408.

About the Authors

Yonggi Cho founded Yoido Full Gospel Church, which is the world's largest church. The church was founded in a tent with five members in May of 1958, and for fifty-nine years it has been guided by the Holy Spirit and has grown to approximately eight hundred thousand members (including twenty satellite churches). The church continues to grow as a congregation that is focused on sharing God's love and happiness with neighbors and the whole world. Dr. Cho convincingly teaches principles in dynamic faith in Jesus Christ, fourth-dimension spirituality, and dependence on the Holy Spirit, and he brings hope in all of life's challenges.

Wayde Goodall is passionate about helping Christians and Christian leaders grow in their faith and understand life disciplines and principles that encourage life balance and dynamic spiritual growth. He has a unique forty-year background in leadership, counseling, consulting, coaching, strategic planning and development, and practical theology. Dr. Goodall provides his clients with unique advantages in understanding personal Christian growth, as well as healthy leadership principles. He has authored or coauthored seventeen books and developed a nationally awarded clergy magazine. Dr. Goodall and his wife, Rosalyn, have served as pastors of three churches and are frequent speakers at denominational, church, and government events (domestically and internationally).